UNIQUE
New Mexico

A Guide to the State's Quirks, Charisma, and Character

Sarah Lovett

John Muir Publications
Santa Fe, New Mexico

Special thanks to Tim Thompson, Murrae Haynes, Anne Sahlin, Orlando Romero and the Museum of New Mexico, Al Regensberg, archivist, Joy Stickney and *New Mexico Magazine*, Ulysses Abeita, Isleta Pueblo, Lynne McKelvey, Abbie and Bob Casias, Suzanne Johnson, Anna Appleby, Peggy van Hulsteyn, LeRoy Sanchez, Los Alamos National Laboratories, Roy vanderAa, Gary M. Stolz, Ronald Latimer, Richard M. Chamberlin, Economic Field Geogologist, New Mexico Bureau of Mines and Mineral Resources, New Mexico Film Commission, and Joe Bowlin and the Billy the Kid Outlaw Gang, Inc. Historical Society.

John Muir Publications, P.O. Box 613, Santa Fe, New Mexico 87504
Cover © 1993 by John Muir Publications
All rights reserved. Published 1993.
Printed in the United States of America

First edition. First printing May 1993.

Library of Congress Cataloging-in-Publication Data
Lovett, Sarah, 1953-
    Unique New Mexico : a guide to the state's quirks, charisma, and
    character / Sarah Lovett.
       p.   cm.
    Includes index.
    ISBN 1-56261-102-X : $10.95
      1. New Mexico—Guidebooks. 2. New Mexico—Miscellanea—
    Guidebooks.   I. Title.
    F794.3.L68 1993   93-3003
    917.890453—dc20   CIP

Design and Typography: Ken Wilson
Illustrations: Chris Brigman
Typeface: Belwe, Oz Handicraft
Printer: Malloy Lithographing

Distributed to the book trade by
W. W. Norton & Co.
New York, New York

Front cover photo © Leo de Wys Inc./Steve Vidler
Front cover photo inset © Leo de Wys Inc./Steve Vidler
Back cover photo © Marc Nohl, NM Economic & Tourism Dept.

CONTENTS

INTRODUCTION

Nothing but blue skies, wide open spaces, and spicy food—that's New Mexico, right? Walk through a field of red chile, or sit on top of a vast mesa, and you know you're in the Land of Enchantment. Of course, there are many things still to be discovered about unique New Mexico. For instance, did you know that New Mexico is one of the oldest places of human habitation in North America? And that it's the largest chile producer in the nation? Did you ever imagine that the state produces award-winning wines? And that the white water of the Upper Box of the Rio Grande is like no other river-rafting run in the world? And did you realize that while you're in Taos, you can back-pack into the wilderness—by llama, no less.

Unique New Mexico is a compilation of fascinating destinations, key facts, interesting charts, quick-reference maps, and fun trivia. Where else can you find a recipe for green chile cake, a map of the state's wineries and breweries, lists of the most off-beat fiestas, a map of the pueblos, a guide to haunted houses and hotels, and directions for making your own adobe bricks?

You can open to any page and find readable, entertaining information bites. The index guides you to specific topics and sites. The contents is set up to give you an idea of what subjects each section covers. However you choose to use this book, you'll soon discover what is unique about New Mexico. ✒

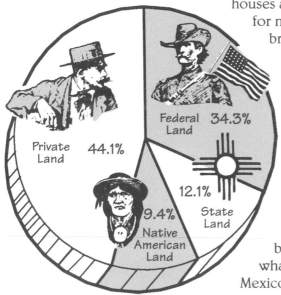

Federal Land   34.3%

Private Land   44.1%

12.1%   State Land

9.4%   Native American Land

Who Owns New Mexico?

Pining for Nuts

Three centuries ago, when Spanish priests first journeyed into the Southwest, they found Native Americans using piñon (pine) nuts as a multipurpose food. Much like the pignoli of southern Europe, piñon nuts were eaten like seeds, and they were also used to thicken and flavor stews. Today, if you're traveling through New Mexico during late spring or early summer, you may see cars parked along the roadside in piñon-studded areas. Collectors sometimes spread a blanket on the ground to catch nuts shaken from a tree.

The piñon is the state tree. This venerable member of the *Plantae* kingdom can grow for hundreds of years, but because piñon is a slow-burning wood, it has long been popular for fires. It's also slow growing, and it's difficult to replant deforested areas. When you're wintering in the state, remember that the heavenly smell of a piñon fire is expensive environmentally. 🌰

Timothy Thompson

A piñon tree growing out of the rocks at Echo Amphitheater, north of Abiquiu

New Mexico

Population:
1,515,069

Area:
121,593 sq. miles

State Capital:
Santa Fe

Nickname: Land of Enchantment

Date of Statehood: 1912

Highest Elevation: Wheeler Peak,
13,161 ft.

State Flower:
Yucca

State Bird:
Roadrunner

State Vegetables:
Chile, Frijoles

State fossil:
Coelophysis

State Gem:
Turquoise

THEN AND NOW

In the Beginning: 100 Million Years Ago to A.D. 1

The Archaic

As the last great Ice Age was easing off, humans journeyed from Asia into North America. Giant glaciers lowered the oceans, and what is now the Bering Strait was dry land, passable on foot. No doubt it proved a long, fatiguing hike. Various sites in New Mexico offer visitors a glimpse of archaic life.

1) Folsom Museum:

Folsom man was a mighty hunter who used stone-chipped tools to slaughter and butcher his prey: mammoths, mastodons, elephants, four-toed horses, and giant sloths. The museum, near the discovery site of flint points embedded in mammoth bones, is the place to see fossils, flint points, and other artifacts that date back at least 13,000 years. *FYI:* Main St., Folsom, off NM325; 505-278-2122.

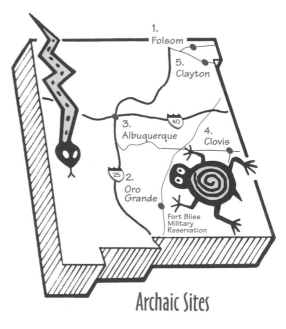

Archaic Sites

2) Pendejo Cave: This small, north-facing cave in Rough Canyon east of Oro Grande town on the Fort Bliss firing range seems to have been a one-stop hunting and butchering spot for Oro Grande man. Flint tools, burned hearthstones, and blackened bones of tapirs, camels, and saber-tooth tigers have convinced some archaeologists that humans lived here as long as 39,000 years ago. *Pendejo* means "stupid" or "dull" in Spanish. *FYI:* Andover Foundation for Archaeological Research, 1 Woodland Rd., Andover, MA 01810; 508-470-0840.

3) Sandia Cave: The first evidence of Sandia man was the discovery of a giant sloth's claw (an animal that has been extinct for 10,000 years) by a troop of Boy Scouts in 1927. The view the ancients had from the mountain's crest was much as it is today—Mount Taylor rising from the basin in the distance, the Socorro Mountains to the southwest, and to the northwest, the Jemez range—all created from volcanic activity long before Sandia man existed. *FYI:* off NM165, east of Albuquerque.

4) Blackwater Draw archaeological site gives visitors a glimpse of Clovis culture Pleistocene hunters. Depressions in the ground are thought to be 10,000 years old. These shafts might have been dug to reach water during drought years. **Blackwater Draw Museum**, located near the site, displays fossils, artifacts, and geologic exhibits related to the Clovis, Folsom, and Portales cultures. *FYI:* southwest of Clovis, on US70 south; 505-562-2202.

5) Clayton Dinosaur Trackway at Clayton Lake State Park takes you back 100 million years, when most of New Mexico was a vast, shallow sea. Five hundred fossilized tracks, belonging to at least eight species of dinosaurs, can be seen on the lake's spillway. Nearby, the town of Clayton, founded in 1887, was a major shipping center for cattle from the Pecos Valley and the Texas Panhandle. Population 2,968; elevation 4,969 ft. *FYI:* Clayton visitors information: 505-374-9253. 🐾

Prehistoric Trivia

☛ **Prehistoric life had its pleasures and its pains. There may have been more quality time for art and contemplation, but a typical life span in A.D. 900 was 35 years or less, and toothaches and arthritis were common complaints.**

☛ **Anasazi is a Navajo word that loosely translates as "the ancient enemies."**

☛ **The Anasazi were accomplished traders: the artifacts found at Aztec ruins included jewelry made of California shell, turquoise from Utah, and bronze bells and parrot feathers from Mexico.**

Mark Nohl, courtesy of NM Magazine

Pueblo Bonito, Chaco Culture National Historic Park

A.D. 1-1300

First Culture

Anasazi and **Mogollon** are two names you need to know before you begin trudging off into the desert to admire potsherds and artifacts. Anasazi culture (in what is now northern New Mexico) and Mogollon culture (to the south and west) existed from the beginning of the first century A.D. to the fourteenth century, evolving from the even earlier Basket Makers to Classic Pueblo peoples. During this span of history, these cultures mastered stonemasonry, pottery, surface mining, water control systems, and road engineering.

In the late 1200s, the great pueblos were abandoned. Why? It's still officially a mystery, but climate changes and drought were definite factors. City problems—overpopulation, disease, housing, trade, and environment—all had to be dealt with (unsuccessfully, it seems). It's plausible that the Anasazi and Mogollon peoples drifted away and relocated along the Rio Grande. By the next century, most of the major pueblos that survived into historic times had been established, including Zuñi, Ácoma, Taos, Isleta, and Galisteo.

Back when William the Conqueror was dreaming up the Tower of London and El Cid was battling the Moors in the city of Valencia, Anasazi culture was thriving in communities at Kayenta, Mesa Verde, and Chaco Canyon—the area that is now **Chaco Culture National Historical Park**. Although projectile points discovered at Chaco prove that the area was occupied ten thousand years ago by Paleo-Indians and the Basket Maker people probably began cultivating corn and squash around 1000 B.C., the descendants of the Basket Makers, the Anasazi, did not begin to construct surface dwellings until between A.D. 700 and 900.

During its classic period (beginning in the eleventh century), Chaco became the center of culture and the most impressive prehistoric civilization in the San Juan Basin and the Southwest. The relics found at Chaco reflect the good life—the people created a central government that did not deny democracy—one that lasted twice as long as the United States has to date. *FYI:* on NM57, 30 miles south of NM44, 505-786-7014.🐾

Puye Cliff Dwellings: Be ready to climb a rough trail and scale at least one ladder. These lovely cliff-perched ruins on the Pajarito Plateau are owned by the Tewa-speaking Pueblo of Santa Clara, whose ancestors were its inhabitants. *FYI:* on NM5, off NM30; 505-753-7326.

Bandelier National Monument: These dwellings in Frijoles Canyon were abandoned before historic times, but drought doesn't seem a plausible cause in this river canyon. Theories include invading enemies, internal feuds, and witchcraft. The site is named for Adolph Bandelier, the Swiss-American ethnologist who visited New Mexico in the 1880s. *FYI:* off NM4; 505-672-3861.

Aztec National Monument: Twelfth-century Anasazi (not Aztec!) ruins. The Great Kiva (a circular ceremonial room built underground) has been fully restored. *FYI:* 1-1/2 miles north of Aztec on US550; 505-334-6174.

Maxwell Museum of Anthropology: Culture, art, and history of the American Indian, especially the cultures found within the state. *FYI:* University of New Mexico, Albuquerque; 505-277-4404.

For early humans, the produce department was the great outdoors, stocked only with native plants. You can still find these edibles growing in New Mexico:
wolf berry,
wild rhubarb (poisonous as a mature plant),
lamb's quarters,
pigweed,
buffalo grass,
piñon, and
creosote bush.

1500-1700

New World Blues

Shipwreck and slavery were part of the initiation by fire for New Mexico's first hardy European explorers. ("Invaders" might be a more accurate term if you consider the perspective of native inhabitants.)

In spite of the known hardship and danger involved in exploring northern lands, tales of streets paved with gold in the Seven Cities of Cibola fueled the Europeans' zeal. In 1540, young Francisco Vásquez de Coronado led an expedition of 300 soldiers and 800 Indians north from Mexico. Instead of gold, Coronado found a "huddle of mud huts" and resistance from the Zuñi pueblos. He defeated the Zuñis and captured their villages, but a precedent had been set, and fierce pueblo resistance continued throughout the Spanish period.

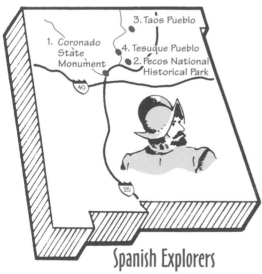

Spanish Explorers

1) Coronado State Monument and Park: On his expedition of 1540, Coronado named this valley the Province of Tiguex for its 12 pueblos. The monument contains the ruins of the northernmost pueblo, Kuaua, which was occupied between 1300 and 1700. *FYI:* off NM44 west; 505-867-5351; camping and picnicking info, 505-867-5589.

2) Pecos National Historical Park: At the time of Coronado's expedition, this 5-story, 660-room pueblo accommodated 500 Towa-speaking Indians, who were its inhabitants from about 1450 to 1838. Plagued by marauding Comanches and deadly epidemics, the last 17 pueblo residents finally migrated to Jémez Pueblo in 1838. *FYI:* NM63 south; 505-757-6414.

3) Pueblo de Taos: In 1680, the Pueblo Revolt began here when Popé, the religious leader ousted from San Juan Pueblo by the Spanish, sent out messengers who raced to other pueblos carrying a knotted cord. The knots signified the number of days until the beginning of the uprising. *FYI:* Box 1846, Taos Pueblo, NM 87571; 505-758-9593.

Taos Pueblo circa 1940

DOD #2759, NM Records Center & Archives

4) Pueblo of Tesuque: Established about 1300, this small Tewa-speaking pueblo was first seen by Europeans in 1591. The Tewa pueblos of Tesuque, Nambé, Pojoaque, Santa Clara, San Ildefonso, and San Juan directed the Pueblo Revolt of 1680 which drove the Spanish from New Mexico for 13 years. *FYI:* Route 1, Box 1, Santa Fe, NM 87504; 505-983-2667.

Cultural Exchange

The wheel, metal tools, gunpowder, written language, horses, sheep, pigs, cows, wheat and other cereals, fruit trees, and many vegetables were Spanish contributions to the Southwest. On the down side, they also brought alcohol and diseases—smallpox, whooping cough, measles, and cholera—which devastated the pueblos.

In 1598, Juan de Oñate, a prominent and wealthy citizen of Zacatecas, led an expedition of soldiers, colonists, and Franciscans into New Mexico. On his return in 1605, he camped at the foot of **El Morro** (between Zuñi and Ácoma) and cut his name in stone above the water hole. Oñate was the first European to sign **Inscription Rock**, although it was already adorned with petroglyphs and petrographs. Today, El Morro is a national monument where you can camp and hike. *FYI:* off NM53 west; 505-783-4226.

El Morro National Monument

Mark Nohl, courtesy of NM Magazine

1821-1846

Mexico Rules

Mexico gained independence from Spain on August 24, 1821, under the Treaty of Cordova. With this independence came dominion over what had been Spanish lands. This Mexican period would last for 25 years until Brigadier-General Stephen Watts Kearny hoisted the U.S. flag over the Palace of the Governors in Santa Fe on August 18, 1846. Partly because Mexico was in a state of bedlam—revolution was followed by civil wars and frequent changes in administration—it was a rousing and tumultuous time in the northern frontier of New Mexico.

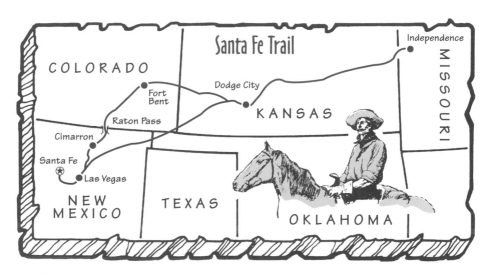

Santa Fe Trail

Mountain Branch of the Santa Fe Trail: Anglos are comparative newcomers to New Mexico. It wasn't until Mexico's revolt from Spain in 1821, and the subsequent opening of the Santa Fe Trail, that foreign U.S. traders were welcomed in Santa Fe. The trail linked Franklin, Missouri, to Santa Fe, New Mexico, and "Stretch out, streeetch ouu-utt!" was the starting command for the two- to three-month trip on Conestoga wagons. A 25-wagon caravan included nearly 300 mules or oxen just to haul the wagons. Mule skinners and bullwhackers earned about $70 a month. Often, dust from large caravans could be seen from a distance of 20 miles. Today, wagon ruts and landmarks still mark the trail.

Clayton Complex: Wagon ruts 150 years old are visible here in Union County, in the northeast corner of the state.

Fort Union National Monument:
The Mexican War (1846–1848) and the discovery of gold in California (1849) caused rush hour along the Old Santa Fe Trail, and Fort Union was established in 1851 as a base for military troops and a rest stop for exhausted travelers. A second star-shaped earthwork was constructed during the American Civil War. Today, visitors see remains of the trail and the second and the third forts, built in 1863. Prerecorded bugle calls—from reveille to bed check—sound daily. *FYI.* NM161 north; 505-425-8025.

Santa Fe Plaza: This was the end of both the Santa Fe Trail from Missouri and the Camino Real from Mexico. Hitching posts and watering troughs (still on the northwest corner) are reminders of the trail's rowdy heyday. The plaza was laid out in 1610 by directive of the king of Spain. It has served as town center for almost four centuries. It probably doubled as a bull-ring—at least very briefly—in 1821, when Mexico gained independence from Spain. Today, you'll dodge skaters and low riders instead of bulls. &

Trail and Travel Trivia

☛ **On the Old Santa Fe Trail, fully loaded, ox-driven trains could average 12 to 15 miles each day traveling almost 2 miles per hour. Mule trains were speedier, covering roughly 20 miles each day. On the return trip, empty wagons moved faster.**

☛ **Although travelers suffered dreadfully from scurvy as they traveled the Old Santa Fe Trail, they found relief in New Mexico by consuming great amounts of chile, which is rich in vitamin C.**

☛ **In 1846, Kearny marched his troops northward along the Rio Grande, officially notifying each settlement that New Mexico was now a territory of the U.S. and the people its citizens. It's rumored that by the time he reached the Santa Fe Plaza, festivities included firing dirty socks from a cannon (due to lack of ready ammunition rather than a penchant for gamy laundry).**

Fort Union was established in 1851

Mark Nohl, courtesy of NM Magazine

1861-1880s

Both Civil Wars

When Civil War erupted in 1861, it seemed as if the Confederates would annex New Mexico with ease. At the bottom of the state, a group of recent immigrants from Texas created a core of Southern sympathizers, and the majority of New Mexico's ranking military officers defected to the South early on. In the summer of 1861, Confederate Army Lt. Col. John R. Baylor marched into the territory near Mesilla, chased Union troops to Organ Pass, and forced them to surrender. In August of the same year, he declared New Mexico south of the 34th parallel a territory of Arizona. New Mexico was not the site of major fighting, but the battles that did occur were strategically important.

On February 21, 1862, a Confederate force of Texas volunteers under the command of Gen. H. H. Sibley defeated Union forces led by Col. E. R. S. Canby at the **Battle of Valverde**. This was the first major battle of the Civil War on New Mexican soil. (Valverde Battlefield is now buried under four feet of silt from the Elephant Butte dam project.)

On March 27 and 28, 1862, a regiment of Colorado volunteer soldiers and regular troops from Fort Union defeated Sibley's band of Confederate Rebels at the **Battle of Glorieta Pass** above the mouth of Apache Canyon. This battle came to be known as the Gettysburg of the West. *FYI:* 25 miles southeast of Santa Fe on I-25. 🐃

"The Long Walk" of 1863

McNitt Collection, #5702 NM Records Center & Archives

Kit (Christopher) Carson (1809-1868)

By 1863, a reluctant Kit Carson was placed in charge of a campaign to break the 10,000-strong Navajo tribe. A systematic program of agricultural devastation ruined the tribe's economy. In January 1864, exhausted and starving Navajos surrendered to Kit Carson at Canyon de Chelly, Arizona. They were then forced to leave their homeland. Although Carson has fared badly with some historians, others say he was a man who respected and admired the Navajos and who participated in the anti-Indian campaign reluctantly. The **Kit Carson Home and Historical Museum**, Taos, was the site of his residence from 1843 (when he married Josefa Jaramillo) until his death in 1868. It has some original furnishings and a good bookstore for Southwest literature. *FYI:* Kit Carson Rd., Taos; 505-758-4741.

Neg # 58388, Museum of New Mexico

Indian Wars

In the 1860s, New Mexico and Arizona were the settings for appalling Indian Wars that lasted longer than anywhere else in the nation. As the Civil War depleted troops in the territory, Indians geared up for violent confrontation in their homeland to drive non-Indians out. The commander of the State's Military Department, Brig. Gen. James Carleton, initiated a harsh policy against hostile tribes.

By March 1863, more than 400 Apache warriors and their families were placed under guard at Fort Sumner at the Bosque Redondo Indian Reservation (now **Fort Sumner State Monument**). The U.S. government interned almost 10,000 Navajos and Apaches during a five-year period of disease, malnutrition, and food and fuel shortages. This failed and harrowing relocation of Indians from their homelands to the fort is known as "The Long Walk." *FYI:* Fort Sumner State Monument, Billy the Kid Rd., off US60/84, Fort Sumner; 505-355-2573.

1846-1912, Territorial Period

Outlaws, Rogues, Rascals, Rustlers, and Other Good Ol' Boys

Territorial Governor Miguel Antonio Otero noted in his memoirs that "New Mexico was located so as to receive the backwash from two streams. From one side Texas, Kansas, Colorado, and the Indian Territory deposited their flotsam and jetsam of humanity, while from the other side Utah, Arizona, and California spewed their human refuse. New Mexico became a sort of catch basin for this type." While the governor was either a realist or a pessimist depending on your view of your fellow human beings, it would be difficult to dispute the fact that territorial days were rowdy, wild, and, sometimes, extremely dangerous. 🙠

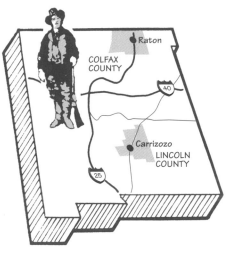

Land Wars

After the 1869 sale of the two-million-acre Maxwell Land Grant, farmers, homesteaders, cattlemen, and miners fought for control of the vast region. It took years of bloody conflict before the **Colfax County War** (1875-1878) finally ended. Murder, shoot-outs, vigilante lynchings, and general chaos led to the removal from office of Territorial Governor Samuel B. Axtell in 1878. Other players included the infamous Texas gunman, Clay Allison, and the Santa Fe Ring, an opprobrious and dominating Republican political machine.

The **Lincoln County War** (1878-1881) of southern New Mexico was even more sensational than the Colfax County War. Lincoln County, the largest in the U.S. with 27,000 square miles, inspired a law-less war between merchants, homesteaders, and cattlemen. Members of the criminal element (including Billy the Kid) were attracted from all over the Southwest like sharks to blood.

Black Jack Ketchum was a train robber from the Clayton area who literally lost his head when he was hanged from the gallows on April 26, 1901. His hideout was located in Turkey Creek Canyon near the town of Cimarron.

Billy the Kid (1859-1881)

The Kid was born Henry McCarty in the Big Apple. Young Henry traveled west with his widowed mother and witnessed her marriage to William H. Antrim at Santa Fe on March 1, 1873. At that time, "Billy" Antrim was 14 years old. A year later, when his mother died in Silver City, Billy began his infamous career. He went to jail in Grant County after the burglary of a Chinese laundry but escaped by scrambling up a chimney and crossing the territorial line to take refuge in Arizona. Until he was gunned down by Sheriff Pat Garrett on July 14, 1881, this young outlaw was variously known as Kid Antrim, William H. Bonney, El Chivo, and The Kid. **FYI:** Billy the Kid Outlaw Gang, Inc., Historical Society, P.O. Box 1881, Taiban, NM 88134; 505-355-2555. Lincoln County Heritage Trust, P.O. Box 98, Lincoln, NM 88338; 505-653-4025.

Tintype courtesy of Lincoln County Heritage Trust

According to Territorial death warrants, "dead, dead, dead," was the state a condemned prisoner must reach before the noose could be removed from his or her unfortunate neck. Between 1846 and 1912, hanging was the official method of execution, and more than 100 persons were condemned to this death by territorial courts. While not every conviction was carried out, unofficial lynchings (by mobs known as "Judge Lynch") made up the difference. 🐎

Territorial Hangings

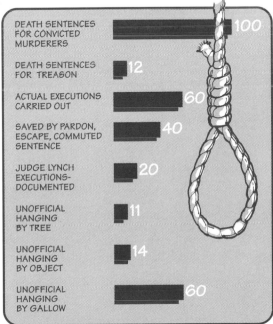

DEATH SENTENCES FOR CONVICTED MURDERERS	100
DEATH SENTENCES FOR TREASON	12
ACTUAL EXECUTIONS CARRIED OUT	60
SAVED BY PARDON, ESCAPE, COMMUTED SENTENCE	40
JUDGE LYNCH EXECUTIONS- DOCUMENTED	20
UNOFFICIAL HANGING BY TREE	11
UNOFFICIAL HANGING BY OBJECT	14
UNOFFICIAL HANGING BY GALLOW	60

1860-1900s

Miners and Railroaders

Post-Civil War New Mexico was abuzz with railroad, mineral, and land fever. This was the beginning of an unprecedented boom, when the future held seemingly endless opportunity if you were one of the territory's 15,000 Anglo-Americans. The late 1860s brought the telegraph and major gold and silver strikes; the late 1870s and early 1880s brought the railroad.

Although the territory's mining boom was brief—and left ghost towns in its wake—it primed the economy. Towns like Hillsboro, Chloride, and White Oaks exploded overnight and then bit the dust. Today, they are great places to explore.

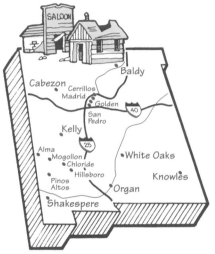

A few of New Mexico's many ghost towns may be visited today

New Mexico's railroad boom was brief; almost one-third of the state's total track mileage was laid between 1879 and 1881. Painted Sadies, rowdy construction crews, cattlemen and sheepherders, Harvey House Girls, doctors, lawyers, and determined purveyors of just about anything crooked or straight followed the tracks.

Along with advances of civilization like telephones and trolley cars, El Diablo brought Doc Holliday and Jesse James to Las Vegas. The Montezuma Castle (now a World College campus) and the Plaza Hotel owe their existence to the railroad. Over 900 structures in the **Las Vegas Historic District** are listed with the National Register of Historic Places. *FYI:* 505-425-8631 or 800-832-5947.

Unlike the boom in Las Vegas, "New Town" **Albuquerque** chugged off to a slow start and didn't speed up until 1881. Hotels, stores, saloons, gambling halls, opium dens, and a red-light district all grew up like weeds surrounding the depot. *FYI:* Central Ave. between First and Third sts., Albuquerque; 505-243-3696 or 800-284-2282.

These days, most people come to Santa Fe on Interstate 25, but it's still possible to arrive by train. The **Lamy Depot** is 18 miles to the southwest of Santa Fe, and it is similar in style to other depots throughout the state.

First, Second, Third—these streets in **Raton's Historical District** are loaded with 70 restored buildings that date to the town's railroad days. Victorian buildings include the sandstone Palace Hotel and Shuler Theater. FYI: 505-445-3689 or 800-638-6161. The **Raton Museum** has RR, mining, and ranching exhibits. *FYI:* 216 S. First, Raton; 505-445-8979. ❧

Fortunately for those of us who came too late to experience steam fever, the **Cumbres and Toltec Scenic Railroad** is still huffing and puffing along 64 scenic miles between Chama, New Mexico, and Antonito, Colorado. This authentic narrow gauge was built in 1880 by the Denver and Rio Grande Railway Company. *FYI:* Chama Depot, downtown on NM 17; 505-756-2151.

Mark Nohl, courtesy of NM Magazine

The Cumbres and Toltec Scenic Railroad

Will Rogers once claimed that Fred Harvey and his girls "kept the West in food and wives." Harvey, a young British entrepreneur, built his empire on good eats and smart service. By the early 1900s, there were a dozen Harvey establishments in New Mexico renowned for fresh pie, hot coffee, and a vast work force of attractive young women. Legend has it that 20,000 Harvey Girls moved on to join cowboys and ranchers in marriages that produced 4,000 babies who grew up to be called Fred or Harvey, or both. The **Montezuma Hotel** and the **Castaneda Hotel**, Las Vegas, and the **Clovis Hotel**, Clovis, were part of the Harvey chain. *FYI:* Las Vegas visitors information, 505-425-8631; or Clovis visitors information, 505-763-3435.

Modern Times

Courtesy of Los Alamos National Laboratory

The first atomic test explosion occurred on July 16, 1945, at Trinity Site

At 5:29.45 a.m., July 16, 1945, the first atomic test explosion—Project Trinity—took place at **Trinity Site**. "Fat Man" was the bomb developed by the Manhattan Project at Los Alamos Scientific Laboratories after more than two years of top-secret research.

The site, located in the north central section of the 4,000-square-mile White Sands Proving Ground (now **White Sands Missile Range**) was chosen for its remoteness. During WW II it was used by the War Department as a bombing range.

Fat Man was set atop a 100-foot steel tower, while Ground Zero was at the base of the tower. On detonation, the flash was seen as far away as Santa Fe and El Paso, and windows shattered in Silver City, 120 miles distant. Sand fused by the heat of the Trinity blast earned the name Trinitite. The site is open to the public twice a year by tour, the first Saturdays in April and October. *FYI:* 800-826-0294 (in New Mexico) or 505-437-6120 (out of state). 🐌

Los Alamos, one of New Mexico's youngest cities, is situated near ancient Indian sites on the Pajarito Plateau. In 1942, the Manhattan Project occupied a boys' ranch school here. The **Los Alamos Historical Museum** has exhibits on the Manhattan Project and area history. *FYI:* 1921 Juniper; 505-662-6272 or 662-4493. The town is also home to **Los Alamos National Laboratories**, a center for nuclear and other scientific research—and site of a salvage sale every Thursday at noon. *FYI:* Los Alamos visitors information; 505-662-8105.

Route 66 through Albuquerque, circa 1940

Nineteen-ninety-two was the 66th anniversary of the nation's most famous highway, **Route 66**. The 2,200-mile route from Chicago to Los Angeles traversed New Mexico by what is now I-40. 🐚

Travel west on US60 a dozen miles from Magdalena and, suddenly, the 27 two-and-a-half-ton dish antennas that make up the world's largest radio telescope appear in a cluster that makes you think of B-movie science fiction. In fact, this is the **Very Large Array**, the world's largest radio telescopes. The National Radio Astronomy Observatory operates then under contract with the National Science Foundation.

The Very Large Array, the world's largest radio telescopes, on the Plains of St. Augustine

NATIVE CULTURES

Native Americans

Long before Christopher Columbus arrived in the New World, the people he called Indians were constructing towns, building roads and irrigation systems, and trading for goods. Although Spanish invaders forced the pueblos to adopt Catholicism, Native Americans held onto their own spiritual traditions. Ultimately, a unique mix of Spanish and Pueblo cultures evolved. Today, Navajo, Apache, and Pueblo people live under sovereign rule on their own land.

The ancestral line of contemporary Pueblo peoples can be traced back to New Mexico's late prehistoric groups. Spanish explorers found at least 80 pueblos when they arrived in 1540. At present, there are 19 pueblos in the state, and they represent three major Native American language groups: Zuñi, Keres, and Tenoan.

Apache and Navajo—Athabascan groups—are newer arrivals since they settled in New Mexico some 1,500 years after the first Pueblo peoples. ❧

Do's and Don'ts

Non-Native Americans are welcome to visit pueblo and tribal land to attend those ceremonials open to the public and to appreciate (and sometimes purchase) beautifully crafted pottery, jewelry, weaving, and other traditional arts. Each tribe has its own regulations. When in doubt, use common courtesy. At ceremonials, don't applaud or talk to dancers during the performance. Find out if you need a permit for photographs, video cameras, audio cassettes, or sketching. (Cameras may be prohibited.) Do not wander into nonpublic buildings or off designated paths. If you are invited into someone's home, don't overstay your welcome. Traditional dances and feast days are scheduled almost every month. Call ahead for information.

Although Santa Fe (established 1610) is considered the oldest capital city in the United States, its foundations are laid on an ancient Indian pueblo that archaeologists have identified as Kuapoge, "the place of shell beads near the water." Early Native Americans who settled in the

Ceremonial dancers at the Santa Fe Indian Market

surrounding hills developed sophisticated techniques of weaving and clay work and architectural skills suited to the region's arid climate. Today, Native Americans sell jewelry, ceramics, and fresh baked bread under the portal of the Palace of the Governors. 🥖

Dr. Pablo Abeita (1871-1940)

One of **Isleta Pueblo**'s most interesting and eminent residents, Dr. Pablo Abeita was a spokesman for Native American rights in the state and in Washington, D.C. He was well-known for his wry wit and his colorful speeches and letters that criticized ill-advised Indian Bureau policies and ridiculed ignorant Anglo assumptions about Native Americans. Fluent and literate in Spanish and English, Abeita also spoke his native language. He was awarded honorary degrees in ancient history and philosophy from St. Michael's College (now the College of Santa Fe). Pablo Abeita married Maria Delores Abeita and had five sons. He served as governor of Isleta Pueblo, and he was also a judge for the tribal court.

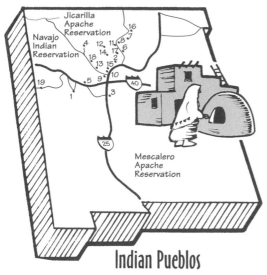

Jicarilla Apache Reservation

Navajo Indian Reservation

Mescalero Apache Reservation

Indian Pueblos

Inhabitants of New Mexico's pueblos are direct descendants of the late prehistoric cultures, Mogollon and Anasazi. Pueblos are still vital cultural centers, each with its own identity, language, and customs. At most times, visitors are welcome, but it's a good idea to call ahead. *FYI:* Eight Northern Indian Pueblos Council, Tourism Department: 505-852-4265.

1) Ácoma Pueblo and San Esteban del Rey de Ácoma:

Situated atop a 357-foot mesa for defensive purposes, Ácoma (known as Sky City) has been continuously occupied for at least a thousand years. For much of that time, the only route to the top was by ladders and rough toe- and finger-holds cut into rock. Hurling stones on the heads of invading enemies was an effective form of protection until angry Spanish forces attacked in 1599. Juan de Oñate ordered the major assault after 13 of his men were murdered at Ácoma. By leaping a chasm, soldier (and poet) Gaspar Perez de Villagra and a dozen Spaniards gained access to the pueblo via a southern route. More than 600 Ácomas were killed and almost as many taken prisoner.

The church, considered one of the finest of the old missions, was probably built between 1629 and 1641. Because of its remote location, earth and 40-foot vigas cut from the Cebolleta Mountains 30 miles away were hauled up from the valley. Long before the construction of the church, Ácomas had been collecting earth for adobe from the plains in buffalo hide bags. *FYI:* 12 miles off I-40; 505-252-1139.

2) Cochiti Pueblo:

The very first and now famous Storyteller figure was made at the Keresan pueblo of Cochiti by potter Helen Cordero in the 1960s. Traditional drums, as well as pottery and jewelry, are a specialty of Cochiti. The pueblo also holds the lease on the land under the town of Cochiti Lake, the 18-hole golf course, the swimming pool, the marina, and tennis courts. *FYI:* west of I-25 and roughly 45 miles north of Albuquerque or 25 miles south of Santa Fe; no admission fee, no cameras; 505-465-2244.

3) Isleta Pueblo: Most members of Isleta—the largest Tiwa-speaking pueblo—live in Albuquerque, but some run businesses on the reservation or work at the bingo hall or at fishing and camping areas. Artisans are famed for their polychrome pots of brown and orange designs against a white-slip background. Two annual feast days in honor of Saint Augustine: August 28 and September 4. *FYI:* 13 miles south of Albuquerque off I-25; 505-869-3111.

Gathering Culture

Native American tribes from the United States, Canada, and Mexico come together by invitation during the **Inter-Tribal Indian Ceremonial** held each August four miles east of Gallup. Ten million dollars worth of art and craft work is on display by more than 1,000 Indian artists. Ceremonial dances, rodeos, a powwow, and the juried show are all part of this event held at Red Rock Museum and State Park. *FYI:* Inter-Tribal Indian Ceremony, P.O. Box 1, Church Rock, NM 87311; 505-863-3896.

McNitt Collection #6802 NM State Records & Archives

Dancers at the 1950 Gallup Ceremonial, Gallup

4) Jémez Pueblo: Sculpture, polychrome ceramics, jewelry, moccasins, and drums are all made by Jémez artisans, the only remaining Towa-speaking pueblo after Pecos Pueblo was deserted in the 1830s. The village welcomes outsiders on two feast days, August 2 and November 12, only. The Red Rock Scenic Area (arts, crafts, and food available), Holy Ghost Spring, and Sheep Spring Fish Pond are open to visitors year-round. Fishing and hunting permits are available from the Jémez game warden. *FYI:* northwest of Bernalillo off NM44; 505-834-7359.

5) Laguna Pueblo: These six villages make up the largest Keresan-language pueblo. St. Joseph's is the big feast day (open to visitors), celebrated on September 19. Laguna ceramics resemble nearby Ácoma's geometric, bird, and animal designs in polychrome. Fishing permits for Paguate Reservoir are available at the Laguna Wildlife Conservation Office. The pueblo was formerly the location of one of the world's richest uranium mines; a tribal reclamation project is now in progress. *FYI:* 46 miles west of Albuquerque off I-40; 505-552-6654 or 243-7616.

6) Nambé Pueblo: Jewelry, sculpture, weaving, blackware and micaceous ware, and beadwork are created by residents of this Tewa-language pueblo. Los Alamos National Laboratory, the Eight Northern Indian Pueblos Council, and the pueblo recreational complex all provide work for residents. Nambé Falls is the site of the annual July 4 Nambé Waterfall Ceremonial. Also open to the public is the St. Francis of Assisi feast day, October 4. Fishing by permit, camping, and boating on Nambé Lake. *FYI:* 22 miles northeast of Santa Fe off NM503; 505-455-2036. Tribal administration office: 505-455-2304, weekends.

7) Picurís Pueblo: This smallest of the Tiwa-language pueblos has gone through boom and bust since its founding in the 1200s. The 1500s were the pueblo's heyday when it had roughly 3,000 inhabitants, but it was abandoned after the Pueblo Revolt. Refounded in the early eighteenth century, Picurís now has less than 300 tribal members. Artifacts are on view at Picurís Pueblo Enterprise Museum. Arts, crafts, and micaceous pottery are on sale at the visitor center. San Lorenzo Feast Day, August 9-10, is open to the public. *FYI:* north of Española via NM76; 505-587-2957.

8) Pojoaque Pueblo: This Tewa-language pueblo was almost wiped off the map by the consequences of the Pueblo Revolt and a smallpox epidemic in the late 1800s. Antonio Jose Tapia and friends reclaimed

Pojoaque in the 1930s, and today there are roughly 200 pueblo members. The frontage businesses on US84-285 generate tribal income. Jewelry, beadwork, pottery, and embroidery are sold at the visitor center. The Plaza Fiesta—with dancing, a carnival, hot-air balloon rides, and food—is celebrated on the first Saturday in August. *FYI:* 8 miles south of Española on US84-285; 505-455-3460.

9) Sandia Pueblo: Bingo is big business 24 hours a day, 7 days a week at this Tiwa pueblo. Originally known as Nafiat, Sandia was founded in 1300. Tribal arts and crafts are on sale at Bien Mur Indian Market Center (near the intersection of I-25 and Tramway). There is permit fishing at the 40-acre Sandia Lakes Recreation Area. You may rent horses at Los Amigos Stables. St. Anthony Feast Day is June 13. *FYI:* 13 miles north of Albuquerque, east of NM313; 505-867-3317.

10) San Felipe Pueblo: The Green Corn Dance, May 1, is noted for its beauty at this Keresan pueblo. Beadwork and heishi (shell beads) and some pottery are made by pueblo artists. *FYI:* off I-25, roughly 10 miles north of Bernalillo; 505-867-3381.

Courtesy NM Magazine

Dancers at San Felipe Pueblo

11) San Ildefonso Pueblo: The late Maria and Julian Martinez made this pueblo famous for their stunning black pottery with black matte designs. Contemporary pottery makers create redware and polychrome and incised pots. They also carry on and refine the black-on-black tradition as well. Signs in homes alert visitors and browsers to businesses. A museum, trading posts, and visitor center are located at the pueblo. Fishing by permit. San Ildefonso Feast Day is January 23; dances are open to the public. *FYI:* located 22 miles northwest of Santa Fe on NM502; 505-455-3549.

12) San Juan Pueblo: This was the site of the first Spanish capital—called San Juan de los Caballeros by conquistadores—in northern New Spain in 1598. Now headquarters of the Eight Northern Indian Pueblos Council, it also houses the Oke-Oweenge Crafts Cooperative and its display of arts and crafts of the eight northern pueblos, as well as the unique redware pottery of San Juan. The Tewa Restaurant offers traditional Indian fare six days a week. Feast Day is in June. *FYI:* 5 miles north of Española off NM68; 505-852-4400.

13) Santa Ana Pueblo: Most tribal members live outside the old Keresan pueblo of Santa Ana in Bernalillo and the surrounding area. The pueblo is open to the public only on January 1 and 6, Easter, June 24 and 29, July 25-26, and December 25-28. Ta Ma Myia Cooperative Association—displaying polychrome pottery, woven belts, and painting—is located at the new village of Santa Ana. The Prairie Star Restaurant and the 27-hole Valle Grande golf course are also tribally operated. *FYI:* village, 8 miles northwest of Bernalillo on NM44; 505-867-3301.

14) Santa Clara Pueblo: Potters from this Tewa Pueblo near Española create polished redware, carved blackware, and famous melon bowls as well as black-on-black ware and polychrome. Santa Clara's Puye Cliff Dwellings and Top House Ruins are closed on December 25 and during inclement weather. St. Anthony Feast Day and Comanche Dance (June 13) and Santa Clara Feast Day (Aug. 12) are open to the public. Permit hiking, camping, picnicking, and fishing in Santa Clara Canyon. *FYI:* NM30 southwest of Española; 505-753-7326.

15) Santo Domingo Pueblo: Situated near the turquoise mines of Cerrillos, this Keresan pueblo carries on a tradition of heishi and jewelry making. Edging pueblo roads are ramadas where jewelry, silverwork, and ceramics are offered for sale. Santo Domingo Arts and

Crafts Market—artists, food, dances—is held on Labor Day weekend. The Corn Dance is August 4. There is also a small store and museum. *FYI:* off I-25 near Santo Domingo exit; 505-465-2214.

16) Taos Pueblo: The raw earth, multistoried dwellings of this Tiwa pueblo are internationally famous. The pueblo is listed on the National Register of Historic Places, and it was nominated by the World Heritage Commission in Geneva as the 15th American site in the World Heritage Convention. San Geronimo Feast Day is held on September 30 and attracts a crowd. The **Taos Pow Wow** is held on the second weekend in July; almost 50 tribes from the United States and Canada gather here to dance and drum. The powwow's style of tribal dancing originated with Plains tribes but was adopted by past generations of Pueblo Indians. Taos Pueblo offers guided tours in summer. *FYI:* 505-758-9593.

17) Tesuque Pueblo: Artists specialize in micaceous pottery, sculpture, and painting at the smallest of the Tewa-language villages. There is a store where arts and crafts are sold, as well as an RV park. Pueblo bingo begins at 5:00 p.m. There's an early bird special at 6:30, and the main series begins at 7:30 p.m. The pueblo is home to pesticide-free Tesuque Farms. San Diego Feast Day is November 12. *FYI:* Bingo, 505-984-8414; Governor's Office, 505-983-2667.

Mark Nohl, courtesy NM Magazine

anta Fe's **Indian Market** is a "million dollar baby," although no one will say for sure how much money changes hands each August. The work is created by some of the country's most illustrious Native American artists. Weekend crowds are thick, and the work is pricey, but bargains can still be had as the sun begins to set on Sunday. *FYI:* Southwestern Association on Indian Affairs, 509 Camino de los Marquez, Santa Fe, NM 87501; 505-983-5220.

Visitors and residents at Zuñi Pueblo

18) Zia Pueblo: The ancient sun symbol of this Keresan-language village can be seen on the state's license plates and flags since it is now the official state emblem. The Zia bird and double rainbow designs are displayed on many polychrome ceramics. Oil and watercolors are used by Zia painters. August 15 is Our Lady of Assumption Feast Day, celebrated with a Corn Dance. *FYI:* 17 miles northwest of Bernalillo on NM44; 505-867-3304.

19) Zuñi Pueblo: The legendary Seven Cities of Cibola were actually the six original Zuñi pueblos. They were abandoned during the Pueblo Revolt, and the site of the present pueblo was settled in 1699. Zuñi became the first Native American community to administer its own reservation in 1970.

The all-night Shalako ceremony is held in early December, and visitors are allowed in some pueblo homes. Stone-work, inlay, overlay, and "needlepoint" are all styles of Zuñi's famous jewelers. There is permit camping, hunting, and fishing in season. *FYI:* Tribal Fish and Wildlife Department, 505-782-5851; Zuñi Pueblo, 505-782-4481.

Navajo tribal land includes sections of Arizona and Utah in addition to New Mexico, and it covers enough turf to equal the size of West Virginia. The tribe—165,000 Navajos live on the reservation—is the nation's most populous, and about one-third of its members reside in New Mexico. Window Rock, Arizona, is the center of Navajo government and enterprise. The six-day **Shiprock Navajo Fair**, held in early October, is the tribe's oldest and most traditional. In addition to an intertribal powwow, rodeo, and parade, there are livestock shows, country-western dances, farmers' markets, food, and arts and crafts displays. All this is held in conjunction with a Yei-Be-Chai healing ceremony (some of which is open to the public). Navajo jewelry and rugs can be bought at trading posts throughout the reservation. Navajo rugs are famous for their weave and style, which includes Two Grey Hills, Burnt Water, and Crystal. There is plenty of space on the reservation for great fishing, hunting, and camping by permit. *FYI:* Navajo Nation Tourism Department, P.O. Box 663, Window Rock, AZ 86515; 602-871-6436 or 602-871-7371; fax 602-871-7381. For recreational info: Navajo Fish and Wildlife Department, Box 1480, Window Rock, AZ 86515; 602-871-6451 or 602-871-6452. 🐾

Extending from the Colorado border south for roughly 64 miles (crossed twice by the Continental Divide), the **Jicarilla Apache Reservation** offers fishing and hunting in and around its eight lakes (and the Navajo River) by permit. Game seasons—muledeer, elk, turkey, and waterfowl—vary. Camping and cross-country skiing are permitted in season. Basketry, leatherwork, beadwork, and featherwork created by Jicarilla artists are on display at the local museum and gift shop. Go-Jil-Ya Feast Day is September 14-15. The Little Beaver Rodeo and Powwow is usually held the third weekend in July. *FYI:* Jicarilla Natural Resources Dept., P.O. Box 546, Dulce, NM 87528, Museum and Arts & Crafts Center, 505-759-3242, ext. 274.

The 460,000 acres of the **Mescalero Apache Reservation** offer visitors the chance to fish, camp, and hunt in the mountains of south central New Mexico. Silver Lake, Eagle Creek, and Ruidoso recreation areas are located here. The Inn of the Mountain Gods is the place to find Apache artwork, as well as lodging, restaurants, an 18-hole golf course, tennis, horseback riding, and skeet and trap shooting. Ski Apache employs many tribal members and offers great downhill slopes. Tepees are visible on the hillsides during the first weekend in July when the Apache Maidens' Puberty Rites and Rodeo take place. *FYI:* Mescalero Apache Tribe Recreation Area Management; 505-671-4427. Visitor center and museum in the town of Mescalero on US70; 505-671-4494. 🐾

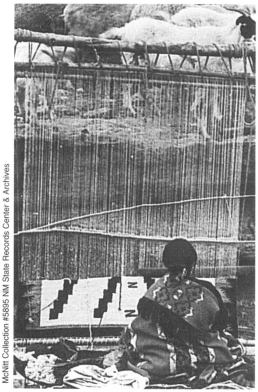

McNitt Collection #5895 NM State Records Center & Archives

A Navajo weaver

Taking Care of Business

The number of Indian-owned businesses rose 64 percent between 1982 and 1987 (compare that with a 14 percent increase for all U.S. businesses). Native Americans bring an edge to the business world. Cohesive communities organize to create efficient production facilities, natural resources are plentiful on many reservations, and "sovereignty" means the suspension of certain local, state, and federal laws on tribal land. Reservations also have the opportunity to cash in on activities not allowed off-reservation.

Bingo is one such activity. One hundred thirteen reservations offer some form of legal gambling; it's a very effective way for tribes to increase their assets, which can then be invested in other projects.

The Trade

Since the late nineteenth century, trading posts have been a bridge, a place of exchange between two cultures—Navajo and Anglo. Eighty years ago, shelves were stocked with canned goods, and the ceiling was hung with tools, tack, baskets, and buckets. Taking just as much space were the rugs, jewelry, wool, and sheep brought in by Navajos to exchange for popular items such as canned red raspberries, tomatoes, peas, and vegetable soup, Arbuckle-brand coffee, and flour.

Stokes Carson raised sheep and traded with Navajos for fifty years. In 1916, Stokes built his own trading post on the edge of the reservation. Although the post has changed hands and has been out of business for periods of time, it still stands. *FYI:* **Carson's** is 20 miles south of Bloomfield on County Rd. 7150; 505-325-3914. Closed Saturday.

Don Batchelor has owned **Nageezi Trading Post** since 1972, but the business dates back to the 1930s. Whether you crave ice cold soda (beer is out because alcohol is not sold on reservation land) or rugs, jewelry, or artwork by local Navajo artists, Nageezi is one-stop shopping on the way to Chaco Canyon. *FYI:* State Route 44 at the turnoff to Chaco Culture National Historical Park; 505-632-3646. 🐚

History Trivia Quiz

1) The community bell at Ácoma Pueblo was taken from Zacatecas, Mexico, in trade for _____.
a) 14 paint ponies
b) 3 cartloads of turquoise
c) 12 captive Apache children

2) The ____ and ____ were the dominant Native American tribes in 19th Century New Mexico.
a) Navajos and Apaches
b) Hopis and Zunis
c) Mogollon and Anasazi

3) A _____ enjoyed by New Mexico's Apaches was made of mescal juice and horse meat.
a) stew b) beverage c) candy

Answers: 1) c 2) a 3) c

Business Trivia

☞ On the Navajo Reservation, more than 60 percent of the population is under the age of 25. An overall reservation jobless rate of more than 30 percent translates to young Navajos out of work. To ease unemployment in the future, tribal business plans include luxury resort developments and collaborations with some of high fashion's most expensive names.

☞ Native American entrepreneurs can take advantage of Futures for Children, an Albuquerque-based nonprofit group whose slogan is, "Education is not the only answer. But without education, there is no answer." Programs include leadership training for teens, a community action program for tribal members, and a motivation program to encourage kids to finish school. *FYI:* 805 Tijeras NW, Albuquerque, NM 87102; 505-247-4700 or 800-545-6843.

Annie Sahlin

Northern New Mexico family in front of their low rider

Village Life

For a taste of the colonial past, drive through the villages of Las Trampas, Truchas, or Chimayó. Many of New Mexico's small towns still retain much of their original character.

Two hundred years after the founding of the village of San Gabriel in 1598, Spanish and Mexican colonists were still settling valleys where an abundance of water, firewood, and land promised a decent life.

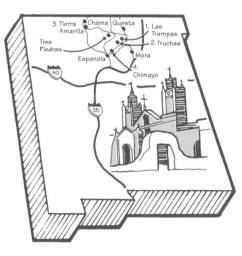

Villages of Northern New Mexico

Sometimes, villages were named for their patron saint, important historical figures, or local families; other village names were approximate translations of Indian words.

Through the end of the seventeenth century and the Pueblo Revolt, Spanish settlements were few and far between. Colonists arrived in greater numbers after the Spanish reconquest of 1692. At that point, a system of land grants was set up by Spain and administered by *alcaldes*, or governors, under colonial law. A few towns and many individual ranches and farms were founded by grants.

rave Art

quiet stop at one of New Mexico's village *camposantos*, or graveyards,
ords visitors a view of select graveyard art—
nate grillwork, gracefully sculpted stones, styl-
ed crosses, designs etched on wood. Each grave-
rd feels a little different; the talents of a single
tisan or village fashion have dictated the style of
e work. Flowers add welcome color—even in
inter—to cemetery earth tones. In simpler times,
ooms were constructed of paper, but technology
ade plastic bouquets possible and everlasting.

ecause these were the days before topographical maps, grant properties
ere defined by trees, mesas, boulders, arroyos, and other natural land-
arks. Later, these rough boundaries caused problems in land disputes
etween Hispanics and Anglo speculators.

) Las Trampas: This village was established in 1751 by Juan de Argüello
nd 12 families from Santa Fe on receipt of a land grant from Governor
omas Vélez Cachupín. The Church of San José de Gracia is one of the
nost graceful survivors from the eighteenth century. Keep your eyes
pen for the rustic viaduct—an old water system—made of tree trunks.
as trampas means "the traps."

) Truchas: Families from Santa Cruz and Chimayó received land on the
Rio Truchas in 1754. Governor Vélez Cachupín insisted that the houses
orm a defensive square with only one entrance to provide protection
rom attack by Plains Indians. Trucha translates as "trout."

) Tierra Amarilla: The Mexican government gave Manuel Martinez and
ellow settlers a large community land grant in 1832. Settlement on the
yellow land" was slowed because of raids by Utes, Navajos, and Jicarilla
Apaches. In 1967, Tierra Amarilla Courthouse was the site of a conflict
between National Guardsmen and land rights activist Reies Lopez Tijerina.

) Chimayó: This village was founded by Spaniards shortly after the reconquest, but the valley had already been occupied by Indians for centuries.
Chimayó has been a Spanish weaving center for more than 250 years. Local
apples and chiles are prized. The Santuario de Chimayó chapel was completed in 1816. It is noted for its simple beauty, and Chimayó earth is
believed by many to have curative powers. Tourist traffic is heavy and
sometimes interferes with those who use the chapel as a place of worship.

*Santa Fe's **Acequia Madre**, "Mother Ditch," dates back to Spanish colonial times. If you trace the ditch today, you find expensive homes instead of corn, chiles, and orchards thriving along it.*

Ditch Boss

Water—its use and division—has always been serious business in the semiarid climate of the Southwest. To sustain corn and bean crops, Spanish settlers employed a system of water management and diversion similar to the method used by some area pueblos. At first, every family maintained its own ditch, but as populations increased, water management became more complicated. The customs, rituals, and laws associated with irrigation still exist today.

The mayordomo de acequia, or ditch boss, of each community works with a three-man commission (all annually elected positions) to ensure that water is distributed fairly and proportionately. Each landowner along the acequia must help build and maintain the system.

Each spring, the acequia must be cleaned and repaired, a back-breaking job. A few communities still maintain the tradition of blessing the acequia after it is overhauled each spring. ⟨🔔

The work of native Hispanic artisans is on view each July at the Santa Fe Plaza during **Spanish Market**. The furniture, weaving, tinwork, colcha stitchery, and carving is among the region's finest. *FYI:* 505-984-6760 or 800-777-CITY.

☛ The annual **Fiesta de Santa Fe** was first established in 1712 to commemorate Don Diego de Vargas's reconquest of New Mexico in 1692 from the Pueblo Indians. The Spanish had dominated New Mexico for 140 years—the Pueblos suffered repression, slavery, and persecution—but the "bloodless reconquest" followed the 1680 Pueblo Revolt. The fiesta, billed as the nation's oldest, has generated controversy within the community. *FYI:* 505-984-6760 or 800-777-CITY.

Fiesta Trivia

☛ **Hispanic fiestas have always been an important part of village life, its religious devotion and celebration. Los Moros y Cristianos (The Moors and Christians) was first performed in New Mexico in 1598 for the residents of San Juan Pueblo by Spanish newcomers. It's still part of Chimayó's annual feast days, December 15-23.** *FYI:* **505-753-2831.**

☛ **Bernalillo observes its feast day with the colorful and somewhat comical Matachines Dance-drama. Although the pageant's origin is a matter of debate, participants are beribboned and sport headdresses covered with flowers, lace, and Christmas bulbs. Fiddles and rattles set the beat for this drama of Christian symbolism. The three-pronged palma embodies Spanish, Moorish, and Aztec influences.** *FYI:* **starts August 10; 505-867-3311, ext. 33.**

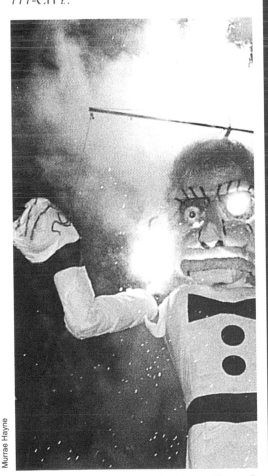

Murrae Hayne

The burning of Zozobra, "Old Man Gloom," kicks off the Santa Fe Fiesta each September

TASTE OF NEW MEXICO

Table Talk

Courtesy of Hatch Chamber of Commerce

Ask anyone about New Mexican cuisine, and they'll undoubtedly say it's hot stuff. The traditional staples of corn, beans, and squash have been spiced up with chile ever since the great-granddaddy of all capsicum peppers was first carried north by an enterprising trader from Bolivia or Peru. Although it's impossible to put an exact date on the chile's arrival in New Mexico, the oldest ancestor of all chiles probably dates back to between 30,000 and 40,000 years ago, maybe even 80,000 years ago. And according to New Mexico State University chile researcher Paul Bosland, some of the same species of chiles that we eat today were consumed by humans in North America 10,000 to 20,000 years ago.

New Mexico chile *is* hot stuff. The pungent pepper's number one heat source is capsaicin, the colorless irritant produced by glands within the fruit. Heat source number two is money. Each year New Mexico's chile crop bolsters the state economy by more than $200 million. Between 20,000 and 30,000 acres of pods are harvested from the 300 or so farms statewide. Chile ranks as the second-largest agricultural crop in terms of cash receipts in the Land of Enchantment (hay is first), and it's the commodity for which New Mexico is known as numero uno in the nation.

Berry, Berry Spicy

Technically, chile is a fruit, a member of the *Solanaceae* family—so are tomatoes, tobacco, petunias, and deadly nightshade—and its pods are actually considered berries. While Chimayó and Española produce special (and famous) chile varieties, almost half of the state's chile is grown in the Mesilla Valley. To celebrate the annual bounty, harvest festivals like the Hatch Chile Festival (in late summer) and the

Whole Enchilada Fiesta at Las Cruces (early autumn) have become popular events in the southern reaches of the state. (See box below.)

Also located smack dab in the middle of capsicum country, New Mexico State University is the institution for chile. Its research activities date back to the turn of the century when Dr. Fabian Garcia was perfecting breeding experiments with the local chile negro and chile colorado as well as the Mexican pasilla chile. The result was the first scientifically developed cultivar, New Mexico No. 9, which was popular with growers until New Mexico No. 6 took the lead in the 1950s. A progeny of that chile, New Mexico No. 6-4, is currently the most popular capsicum in the state, thanks to Fabian Garcia's successors, Roy E. Harper, Roy Nakayama, and Paul Bosland. 🌶

Celebrating the Great Chile

New Mexico has two annual harvest festivals to honor the chile. Both take place in chile country down south.

Hatch Chile Festival: A chile theme parade, spicy food and drink, and prizes for the biggest, hottest, and best are part of the action at the Hatch Airport grounds, in early September. *FYI:* 505-267-5216.

Whole Enchilada Festival: The Downtown Mall in Las Cruces is the place to see the world's largest enchilada—seven feet in diameter!—being cooked each October. Street dancing, parades, children's activities, and a chile cook-off are all part of the entertainment. *FYI:* 800-FIESTAS.

Hot Trivia

☛ **According to one South American legend, chiles arrived on earth as First Man sprinkled them from his testicles over the entreé at the primordial potluck. When the irate attendees recovered from First Man's lack of party manners, they recognized genius and praised him for his contribution.**

☛ **Although Columbus gets credit for misnaming this piquant native staple—he thought it resembled the coveted black pepper of India—he had enough presence of mind to return to Spain with a store of chiles. It seems that within the next 25 years, chiles had reached Goa on the Malabar Coast by way of Lisbon trade routes.**

☛ **If you're in chronic pain, capsaicin might hold relief. The active ingredient in chiles kills pain fibers. On the down side, capsaicin painkillers may burn for hours before the analgesic relief sets in.**

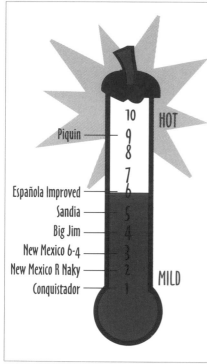

10 HOT
Piquin — 9
8
7
Española Improved — 6
Sandia — 5
Big Jim — 4
New Mexico 6-4 — 3
New Mexico R Naky — 2
Conquistador — 1 MILD

Chile Heat Scale

The capacity of capsaicin to blow your mind—and your taste buds—varies from plant to plant, from region to region. Although most of us are able to intuit whether the chile we're sampling is a 1 or a 10 on nature's heat scale, our opinion isn't science. In the past, humans served as heat-testing guinea pigs when pharmacologist Wilbur L. Scoville developed the Scoville Organoleptic Test. These days, Scoville Units remain, but the humans have been replaced by technology. High-pressure liquid chromatography is currently the preferred method. The heat scale at left is based on figures provided by New Mexico State University, and it should be used as a very general guide to a few of New Mexico's varieties.

Salsa 'til you drop!

In 1990, New Mexico's population was approximately 1,515,069 people. The value of commercial chile salsa consumed that same year was estimated to be $16,468,800. Using a calculator, this computes to an average of $10.87 worth of commercial salsa consumed per capita in 1990. (Estimates courtesy of the NMDA.) 🌶️

Chile harvest

Craving Chile

Scientific studies have shown that each time you sink your teeth into a hot chile, endorphins are released in your body. Could this lead to a Pavlovian-conditioned response of low-grade dependent-type behavior? In other words, after eating chile and feeling happy, could merely looking at chile cheer you up? Frank Estcorn, a professor of psychology at New Mexico Technical University, Socorro, is trying to find out the answer to that question. Research on the use of chile in the treatment of addictive behaviors is also under way at Pennsylvania State University. The question there is: If jalapeño peppers—which rate 5,000 units on the Scoville scale—make you a little happy, could habañero chiles—200,000 Scoville Units!—let you achieve Nirvana? While Professor Estcorn would not state that chile can be effective in treating addictive behaviors, you are free to speculate—and to experiment. 🍮

Mark Nohl, courtesy NM Magazine

Making red chile ristras

How to Put Out an Old Flame

When the worst has happened and you bite into a four-alarm chile, don't wait for the fire trucks. Instead, reach for a remedy that's close at hand—milk! Swish it, slurp it, slug it; although it might be hard to swallow, milk is the number one fire-putter-outer.

Other remedies include yogurt, buttermilk, olive oil, fruit syrup, peanut butter, and even glycerol (but don't swallow this last one).

Plain Talk about Chile

"Red or green?" Some say that's the most commonly asked question in New Mexico. It's certainly the question you'll hear most often in restaurants that serve the state's native dishes. A perfectly legitimate response would be, "Which is hotter today?" Of course, you can't rely on someone else's taste buds without risk; you may get burned. Red chile tends to be milder if both red and green pods are picked from the same cultivar. Unfortunately, that's usually not the case in restaurants. Some people skirt the "red or green" question and order half and half. If you want to go that route, simply say, "Christmas."

To chile, chili, or chilli? In the Land of Enchantment, ask for "chile" to designate the plant, a packet of dried red, or a steaming bowl of red or green. You're safe if you restrict your use of "chili" to refer to chili con carne, as in the Tex-Mex dish (which often comes out of a can in the northern part of the state). Finally, if your roots are Aztec, go ahead and say "chilli."

In the Red

When you pass fields of green chiles, you may wonder what happened to the red ones. Actually, green and red peppers come from the same plant. The first harvest is green; pods left on the plant eventually turn red. Once mature, red pepper pods are dried and ground, and they qualify as the most consumed spice in the world. ❧

A field of chiles ripening in the fall

Mark Nohl, courtesy NM Magazine

Chile at Home

When preparing chile of any color, remember to keep your hands away from your eyes to avoid a painful burning sensation.

Mrs. Chavez's Basic Salsa

1/2 cup red chile powder (not cayenne!)
1/2 cup water
   Measure chile into a small sauce pan and add enough water to make a paste. Add more water until consistency is to your liking. Heat over low flame until liquid just begins to simmer. Remove from heat and serve hot or cool.

Green Chile Cake

12 large chile strips
   (chiles roasted, peeled, seeded)
12 strips longhorn cheese
1 dozen eggs
2 tablespoons flour
   Layer chile strips and cheese in greased shallow baking pan. Mix flour with beaten eggs and pour over. Bake in slow oven until egg mixture is firm. Cut in squares and serve hot. Serves six.

Reproduced from *Pueblo Indian Cookbook*, Phyllis Hughes, ed., copyright 1972, 1979, with permission from Museum of New Mexico Press.

Roasted Corn Salsa

Yield: about 3 cups
five ears of corn in the husk
3/8 cup fresh morels or other wild mushrooms, cleaned and diced
5 tablespoons extra virgin olive oil
1/4 cup diced sun-dried tomatoes, with one tablespoon of their oil
two large poblano chiles, roasted, peeled, seeded, and diced
two tablespoons minced cilantro
two teaspoons marjoram
three cloves garlic, roasted, peeled, and chopped
one tablespoon adobo sauce from canned chipotle chiles in adobo sauce
1/2 teaspoon sherry vinegar
1/2 teaspoon fresh lemon juice
1/2 teaspoon fresh Mexican lime juice
1/2 teaspoon kosher salt
   Roast ears of corn on a baking sheet in a 400 degree oven until the husks begin to blacken (about 15 minutes). Set aside to cool. Meanwhile sautée morels in 1/2 teaspoon of the oil until well cooked, about 10 minutes. Shuck the corn, brush with 1/2 tablespoon of the oil, and grill or broil until the exposed kernels turn a light mahogany, about ten minutes. Let cool and cut the kernels from the ears, shallowly enough to cut through the milky part of the kernel, but not through the cob. You should have about 1 1/2 cups kernels. Mix corn, mushrooms, remaining oil, and the rest of the ingredients together. Serve salsa hot or at room temperature.

"Roasted Corn Salsa" excerpted from *Coyote Cafe*. © 1989 by Mark Miller. Reprinted by permission of Ten Speed Press, P.O. Box 7123, Berkeley, CA 94707.

Traditional horno ovens at Rancho de las Golondrinas

Mark Nohl, courtesy NM Economic & Tourism Dept.

Native Cuisine

While lamb tacos à la cilantro and papaya salsa, red chile egg rolls, and salmon poached in green chile vodka and garnished with piñon nuts might be sampled at a few of New Mexico's trendier eating establishments, most of the state's traditional dishes are simple and delicious.

Corn is a staple of both Hispanic and Native American cuisine, and it's used to make everything from tortillas to frying pan blue corn bread to posole (soft corn kernels, also known as posoli). Chiles, of course, are found in countless variation. Meat dishes include mutton or lamb stew, beef or chicken flautas or enchiladas, and pit-roasted goat *(cabrito)* for special occasions. Pumpkins, squash, berries, and seeds are seasonal favorites. Fry bread pudding (made with raisins, sugar, and cheese), *biscochitos* (sugar cookies made with anise), and natillas pudding satisfy the sweet tooth. And fresh baked native breads are worth a detour. Whether you're sampling the salmon or the mutton stew, do it with a spirit of adventure.

The stalwart tortilla (basically unevolved since pre-Columbian times) still qualifies as the bread staple of the Southwest. **Leona's de Chimayó** is a small Chimayó-based factory that sustains two full-time worker shifts and produces as many as 900 dozen tortillas daily. While the base ingredient of tortillas is blue or yellow cornmeal or

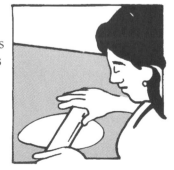

wheat flour, Leona's flavors include maple, chocolate, pesto, and jalapeño. The tortillas are available in stores, restaurants, or by mail, and visitors can sample them at Leona's Restaurant, a lunch stand located next to the Santuario de Chimayó. *FYI:* 505-351-4660 or 800-4LEONAS.

Harvest Festivals

Harvest festivals have been a part of life in New Mexico for as long as humans have been eking out their existence. *FYI:* a calendar of events that includes harvest festivals is available from the New Mexico Department of Tourism, Santa Fe; 505-827-7400.

Each fall, Roosevelt County celebrates the mighty goober with its **Peanut Valley Festival** at Eastern New Mexico State University. This county produces 90 percent of the nation's Valencia peanuts. The Peanut Valley Festival includes a juried peanut art show, a peanut olympics, and a peanut food fair as well as music and crafts. *FYI:* 505-562-2631.

The **Spanish Colonial Harvest** is held each October at **El Rancho de las Golondrinas** (Ranch of the Swallows), one of the loveliest and most historic ranchitos in the Southwest. Las Golondrinas was acquired by Miguel Vega y Coca around 1710—it was the final stop before Santa Fe on the Camino Real—and it remained in his family until 1932. The present owners have restored existing buildings and added others, and the property is beautifully maintained. Listen to music, stroll the countryside, and sample brown bread pulled hot from traditional hornos (outdoor ovens). This is a perfect family event. *FYI:* 15 miles south of Santa Fe; take exit 271 from I-25; 505-471-2261.

Moriarty holds its annual **Pinto Bean Fiesta and Cook-off** each October to celebrate this historic crop. Festivities include a parade, a horseshoe pitching contest, a bean sprout contest, and the crowning of the Bean Queen. Of course, there's a frijole cook-off. *FYI:* 505-832-4087.

The **Farmers and Crafts Market** in Las Cruces is no hayseed stop-and-shop; it's one of the city's freshest tourist attractions, and 300,000 folks visit each year. This market has been in business for more than two decades, and it's now a permanent part of the Las Cruces Downtown Mall on Wednesdays and Saturdays. *FYI:* 800-FIESTAS.

The Fine Art of Viticulture

The art of cultivating the vine is more than three centuries old in New Mexico. By 1662, Franciscan priests were producing a blessed and steady flow of wine for Mass. These venerable Mission grapes (*Vitis vinifera*), cultivated in the Mesilla Valley, predated the first California cuttings by at least 100 years. In fact, the Mission vineyards of southern New Mexico and West Texas qualify as the oldest commercial wine-growing regions in the country.

By 1880, New Mexico was producing a million gallons of wine annually and ranked fifth in the nation in wine production. Although production slumped over the next century, the 400 acres of grapes planted in 1980 have grown to more than 4,000 in 1990, with roughly 70,000 acres suitable for *vinifera* varieties.

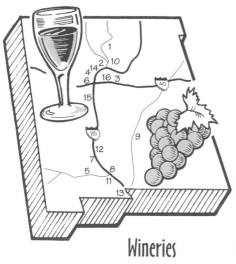

Wineries

Cold nights, a lack of water, and poor soil may not seem like agricultural selling points, but they're a plus for vine growers. The best wine grapes are produced when vines are under stress, and New Mexico's desert climate offers plenty of opportunities for the "S" word. Other advantages include the state's long growing season, sunny climate, irrigation capabilities, and relatively cheap land. The following are some of New Mexico's most established wineries. (Call ahead for hours, information, and appointment, if necessary.)

1) La Chiripada: Highest elevation of any commercial winery in the country; Pat and Mike Johnson, proprietors; 505-579-4437.

2) Balagna Winery: John Balagna, proprietor; 505-672-3678.

3) Madison Winery: Bill and Elise Madison, proprietors; 505-421-8028.

4) Devalmont Winery: Farid Himeur and Laurent Gruet, proprietors; 505-344-4453.

5) St. Clair Vineyards: The state's largest; Patrice Cheurlin, vice president.

6) Anderson Valley Vineyards: Patty Anderson, proprietor; 505-344-7266.

7) German Wine Growers: Chris Wood, general manager; 505-744-5319.

8) Binns Winery: Eddie Binns, proprietor; 505-526-6738.

9) Tularosa Vineyards: Award-winning cabernet sauvignon; David Wickham, proprietor; 505-585-2260.

10) Santa Fe Winery: Len Rosingana, proprietor; 505-753-8100.

11) Blue Teal Tasting Room: Herve Lescombes, proprietor; tasting room, 505-524-0390; winery, 505-542-8881.

12) Domaine Cheurlin Winery: Methode Champenoise; Patrice Cheurlin, proprietor; 505-894-3226 (winery), 505-894-0837 (office).

13) La Viña Winery: Art and Victor Bieganowski, proprietors; 505-882-2092.

14) Las Nutrias Winery: Ken Kendzierski, proprietor; 505-897-7863.

15) Mountain Vista Vineyards: New Mexico Wine Growers Cooperative.

16) Sandia Shadows Winery: Lyle and Barbara Talbot, proprietors; 505-298-8826.

Wine Festivals

Because wine festivals are growing in popularity, only the most well-known events are listed below. For further information, write: New Mexico Vine & Wine Society, Box 26751, Albuquerque, NM 87125.

☛ Mesilla Valley Wine Festival, Memorial Day weekend; 505-524-8521

☛ Santa Fe Wine and Chile Fiesta, September; 505-984-6760 (Write: Santa Fe Wine and Chile Fiesta, Plaza Mercado, 112 W. San Francisco St., Santa Fe, NM 87501)

☛ New Mexico Wine Festival (Bernalillo), Labor Day weekend; 505-867-3311, ext. 33 (Bernalillo City Hall)

Rio Grande Historical Collection, NMSU Library

Wine vat, circa 1894

Norma Klein

Albuquerque beer authority Bob Klein

Brewing Up

By definition, microbreweries are small and the beer is fresh. Because they have a limited capacity for production and distribution, their beers may be available only at the brewery. The microbrewery business in New Mexico is micro. Two of the most visible are located within an easy drive of Santa Fe.

Preston Brewery at Embudo Station claims to be the smallest brewery in the U.S. with a total annual production of 250 barrels. It's also the state's first and only brew pub. There are roughly 20 brews, and four or five are usually on tap. The **Santa Fe Brewing Company** has been brewing up its award-winning Santa Fe Pale Ale in Galisteo since 1987. Although microbrewery beers vary from batch to batch (and special ingredients change frequently), Albuquerque-based freelance writer, beer critic, and taster of more than 900 beers, Bob Klein, has some taste bud impressions of the following New Mexico brews.

Preston Brewery: The brewery is located at the site of the historic **Embudo Station**. This train station complex was built in the 1880s to serve the old Chile Line (part of the Denver & Rio Grande Railroad). These days, you can shop in the **Father Sky Mother Earth Gallery**, have dinner, enjoy a glass of cold beer, or take a dinner float trip down the river. *FYI:* 16 miles north of Española on NM68; 505-852-4707. (Restaurant closed in winter; brew pub open year-round. Call for hours.)

☞ **Rio Grande Green Chile Beer:** This unusual beer has a fresh green chile aroma and taste with a lingering chile-roasted essence; nice mild chile aftertaste with a gentle roll on the tongue. Preston Brewery also offers Rio Grande Ristra (a red chile beer), Narrow Gauge Ale (steam style beer), Railroaders Stout (rich, dark, and chocolatey), and Brewmaster's Reserve (golden dutch style lager) as well as real ginger ale.

Santa Fe Brewing Company: This brewery is located on the outskirts of the village of Galisteo. Many ruins of Tano-speaking pueblos can be explored in the area. *FYI:* tours and tasting; NM41, Galisteo; 505-988-2340.

☞ **Santa Fe Pale Ale:** Ranked second in the pale ale category at the 1991 Great American Beer Festival, Denver, Colorado.
☞ **Barleywine Ale:** Higher in alcohol content than bock, this brew is much more like wine than beer; high in yeastiness, which gives it a fruity citrus flavor; great for wine lovers.
☞ **Santa Fe Old Pojoaque Porter:** Very, very good.

Eske's a Brew Pub

(Taos) is a Southwest-style pub where you can sample six beers on tap including Wanda's Wicked Wheat (25 percent wheat malt beer) and Taos Green Chile Beer. Steve and Wanda Eskeback are owners, operators, and brewmasters at Eske's. This is a comfortable pub where locals and travelers can munch on bangers and mashers (more commonly known as bangers and mash) and green chile stew while sampling seasonal brews.
FYI: 1/2 block southeast of Taos Plaza on 106 Des George's Lane; 505-758-1517.

THE NATURAL WORLD

Four geologic provinces—the Southern Rockies, the Great Plains, the Colorado Plateau, and the Basin and Range—converge within the borders of New Mexico. This means you'll find forests, dunes, mountains, deserts, mesas, and volcanic uplands when you tour the state. This complex geology also means a wealth of life zones, diverse ecosystems, and a varied climate.

Building Earth

The ebb and flow of ancient seas, mountain building, developing deltas and floodplains, faulting, desertification, and violently erupting volcanoes all did their part to shape the state's terra firma. Faulting, which began some thirty million years ago and continues today, created one of the most striking of New Mexico's geologic features, the Rio Grande Rift. This great break in the earth's crust—the work of two extremely deep fault zones—divides the state in rough halves.

The state's most famous river, the Rio Grande, has been the subject of historical chronicles, fiction, movies, and folklore. Coursing the Rio Grande Rift, it developed as a through-flowing river more than two million years ago.

West of the great rift, the Colorado Plateau and volcanic mountains make up New Mexico's northern and southern regions. To the east, from the rift to the borders of Texas and Oklahoma, sweeping plains and soft hills are only occasionally interrupted by river valleys.

The great rip in the earth's crust known as the **Rio Grande Rift** is filled with alluvium and lava. At the bridge spanning the **Rio Grande Gorge**, more than 600 feet of basin fill is visible. *FYI:* 11 miles northwest of Taos on US64.

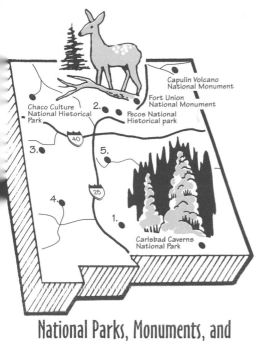

Capulin Volcano National Monument

Fort Union National Monument

Chaco Culture National Historical Park

2. Pecos National Historical park

3.

5.

4.

1.

Carlsbad Caverns National Park

National Parks, Monuments, and Historic Sites

National Parks and Monuments

1) Wind and white gypsum come together at **White Sands National Monument** in the Tularosa Valley to create great dunes. Spring winds (blowing at the optimal speed of 15 miles an hour or more) carry gypsum from Lake Lucero, southwest of White Sands. The groundwater below and around the lake is the source of the gypsum, which crystallizes into chunks of selenite as it reaches the surface. The crystals are broken down by blasting wind, and eventually the sand particles bounce their way to the dunes. Amazing desert adaptations have been made by local plant and animal species that survive in this delicate environment. *FYI:* US70/82 southwest of Alamogordo; 505-479-6124.

2) Bandelier National Monument: This stunning river canyon of volcanic tuff was incised by the Frijoles River. The tuff was deposited by the great eruptions of Jémez volcano; today, **Valles Caldera** (in the heart of the Jémez Mountains) is the only remnant of the volcano. *FYI:* NM4 east of Los Alamos; 505-672-3861.

3) El Morro National Monument: The sheer cliff walls of the bluff are smooth Zuñi sandstone. From the top of the bluff you can see the valley surrounding the **Zuñi Mountains**. *FYI:* east of Ramah on NM53; 505-783-4226.

4) Gila Cliff Dwellings National Monument: The rock here is Gila conglomerate—coarse and pebble-filled—and stems from volcanic ash and lava of the Tertiary volcanic range nearby. Canyon walls were created by uplift and faulting. *FYI:* north of Silver City on NM15; 505-536-9461.

5) The ancient ruins and sixteenth-century churches of **Salinas Pueblo Missions National Monument** are made of local Permian San Andres limestone (Gran Quivira) and red sandstone of the Permian Abo formation (Abo and Quarai). The Estancia Basin was a lake during the Pleistocene. *FYI:* 505-847-2585.

ERA	PERIOD	EPOCH	AGE	DOMINANT LIFE FORMS
CENOZOIC Age of Mammals	Quaternary	Recent		
			.01	
		Pleistocene		
			2	
	Tertiary	Pilocene	5	
		Miocene	24	
		Oligocene	37	
		Eocene	58	
		Paleocene	66	
MESOZOIC Age of Reptiles	Cretaceous		144	
	Jurassic		208	
	Triassic		245	
PALEOZOIC Age of Fishes	Permian		286	
	Pennsyl-vanian		330	
	Mississip-pian		360	
	Devonian		408	
	Silurian		438	
	Ordovician		505	
	Cambrian		570	
	Precambian			

EVENTS IN NEW MEXICO

Present erosion cycle trenches Pleistocene deposits, partly refills Rio Grande Rift valley. Basalt eruptions build cinder cones and lava flows near Grants, Carrizozo, and Capulin.

Cyclic erosion, product of repeated glacial cycles farther north, alternately trenches and fills the Rio Grande Valley. Small mountain glaciers develop in northern New Mexico mountains. Jemez volcano erupts and collapses.

Basins between ranges fill with debris eroded from surrounding mountains. Some drainage integrates: The Rio Grande becomes a through-flowing stream.

Increasing crustal tension creates basins and ranges of southern New Mexico. Intense volcanism builds and destroys many large volcanoes in the southwest part of the state.

The Rio Grande Rift begins to sink between two sets of faults. West of the still-sinking San Juan Basin, plateaus develop.

Debris from the Rocky Mountains fills the San Juan Basin. Mammals diversify, many the ancestors of modern forms.

Continued rise of Rocky Mountains and initial sinking of San Juan Basin accompanies westward drift of continent. Mammals flourish on land. Mineral-bearing intrusions form in parts of the state.

North America breaks away from Europe and starts to drift westward. Briefly, a vast sea covers parts of New Mexico. The Rocky Mountains rise to the north. Finally, a great extinction annihilates many forms of life, ending the Age of Reptiles.

Seas of sand sweep in wide deserts across northern New Mexico. Dinosaurs roam river floodplains and near-shore marshes.

Coastal plain, floodplain, and delta deposits spread across state, their sediments derived from ancestral Rockies. Explosive volcanism adds volcanic ash to these sediments. Dinosaurs appear.

Southern seas advance across much of New Mexico. A large barrier reef develops in the south, followed by drying up of the sea and creation of extensive salt and gypsum deposits. Locally, erosion removes some earlier sedimentary layers.

A southern sea covers much of New Mexico with sand, mud, and limestone. With the rise of the ancestral Rockies, sediments become coarser.

Widespread deposition of fossil-bearing marine limestone is followed by uplift and development of karst topography with solution caverns and sinks.

Marine deposits—limestone and shale—form in shallow seas.

Marine deposits form. Most are later eroded away.

Marine deposits—limestone and shale—form in shallow seas. The first fishes appear.

A western sea advances across the stripped Precambrian surface, depositing sandstone, shale, and limestone. Shellfish are widespread and abundant: the Age of Fishes has begun.

Episodes of mountain-building and volcanism alternate with periods of marine and non-marine sedimentation. Intrusions of granite occurred roughly 1.35 billion years ago. Finally, a long period of erosion flattens the landscape.

From *Roadside Geology of New Mexico* by Halka Chronic, 1987, Mountain Press Publishing Co., P.O. Box 2399, Missoula, MT 59806

Weather the Weather

The vast, geographically complex and varied terrain of New Mexico contributes to the state's diverse climate. In fact, the greatest statewide ranges in temperature in the nation are found here. Northern mountains are cool and wet, while southern deserts are dry and warm. Statewide weather extremes include frequent lightning storms, flash floods, blizzards, droughts, and heat waves.

Weather Chart

Average hours of annual sunshine: 3,700 (southwest); 2,800 (north central)

Highs: 116°F at Orogrande, July 14, 1934, and at Artesia, June 29, 1918.

Hot spots: Alamogordo, Artesia, Carlsbad, Columbus, Florida, Jal, Jornada, Lordsburg, Orogrande, Roswell, White Sands. Highs here average 105°F and higher.

Rain: 11.28 inches in 24 hours, Lake Maloya, May 19, 1955; 16.21 inches in a month, near Portales, May 1941; 62.45 inches in a year, White Tail, 1941.

Floods: 1895, Silver City—a 12-foot wave washed over the town; 1896, Catskill—flash flood swept away 7 miles of railroad track and 25 bridges; 1908, Folsom—18 people died; 1929, San Marcial—flood destroyed the town; 1978, White Sands—5 people died when 8 inches of rain fell in 3 hours; 1988, Albuquerque—7-foot waves caused $3 million in damage and one fatality.

Hail: 1988, Gallup—a building collapsed from 1 foot of hail (up to 1" diameter); 1989, Villanueva—8 inches of hail in one storm.

Cold: 1951, Gavillan— -50°F.

Cold spots: Dulce, Eagle Nest, El Vado, Red River, Tres Piedras, where the average minimum temperature is -20°F or lower.

Snow: 1958, Sandia Crest—30 inches in 24 hours; 1912, Anchor Mine—144 inches in one month; 1911-12, Anchor Mine—483 inches in the season.

Wind: 1987, Albuquerque—124 mph.

Least annual rainfall: 1 inch at Hermanas, 1910

It's a Strike!

Lightning strikes in New Mexico are a deadly business. This state has the highest number of lightning strike deaths per capita in the nation (about 70 between 1959 and 1991). Hikers, golfers, and horseback riders are at risk (metal cleats and shoes on horses and sports enthusiasts act as conductors), and so is anyone else caught outdoors when those powerful electrical discharges are released from thunderclouds. After a bolt strikes a tall object, it may move to a better conductor—like a person. Most victims of lightning strikes are hit by side flashes.

Lightning isn't the only weather hazard in New Mexico. Each year, flash floods destroy hundreds of homes (54 people have died between 1959 and 1991), and tornadoes may cause flooding at the same time that they're ripping the roofs from buildings in their path.

Staying indoors is the safest strategy when electrical storms are raging. If that's not possible, avoid water and isolated trees (or other tall objects). Stay low to the ground, and make yourself into the smallest possible target. 🖎

New Mexico Weather Quiz

1) On the average, during what percentage of all New Mexico's daylight hours can you expect sunshine?
   a) 60% b) 75% c) 88%

2) What New Mexico city recorded 779 days of consecutive sunshine from Dec. 16, 1961, through Feb. 2, 1964?
   a) Truchas b) Farmington
   c) Albuquerque

3) What New Mexico city recorded temperatures of 90° and higher for 64 consecutive days in 1980?
   a) Albuquerque b) Chama
   c) Raton

4) On the average, how many tornadoes strike New Mexico in one year?
   a) 3 b) 8 c) 16

5) In what year did 18 tornadoes strike New Mexico?
   a) 1990 b) 1879 c) 1972

Answers: 1) b 2) c 3) a 4) b 5) c

Weather Trivia

☞ **More people survive lightning strikes than die from them.**
☞ **The electrochemical repository known as the human body is physiologically altered when struck by an electrical discharge: burns, seizures, respiratory and cardiac arrest, muscular contraction, dehydration, and broken bones are the most common repercussions.**

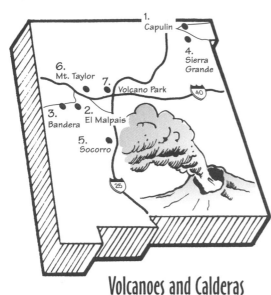

Volcanoes and Calderas

Dormant or Active

1) Travel back in time 10,000 years to the final days of a fiery volcanic eruption, when ash, cinder, and molten lava created an almost perfect mountain. **Capulin Mountain National Monument**, in northeastern New Mexico, is one of the nicest places in the world where you can walk into a volcanic crater. Wildflowers, mountain mahogany, porcupines, and mule deer are all part of the picture.

The two-mile drive up the crater takes minutes, and the spiraling road is steep, with a breathtaking drop-off. Trails lead to the bottom of the crater and also follow the rim. From the highest rim point, you can see Oklahoma, Texas, and Colorado. Remember, Capulin's future is unpredictable. Scientists classify any volcano 25,000 years old or less as potentially active, so young Capulin is dormant, not extinct. *FYI:* 12 miles west of Des Moines by US64/87 and NM325; 505-278-2201.

2) El Malpais National Conservation Area: Here you'll find 262,000 acres of lava flows, cinder cones, fascinating rock formations, and wilderness, all managed by the Bureau of Land Management. *FYI:* visitors center, 620 E. Santa Fe Ave., Grants; conservation area is 10 miles south of Grants via I-40 and NM117; 505-285-5406.

3) Bandera Crater and Ice Caves: The crater is an 800-foot volcanic cone, and the ice caves (containing 12- to 20-foot-thick ice deposits) are part of a 17-mile lava tube. *FYI:* off NM53, 25 miles southwest of Grants; 505-783-4303.

4) Sierra Grande (one of the state's largest volcanoes) is a shield volcano and can

Mark Nohl,courtesy NM Magazine

Lava tube entrance, El Malpais

be seen from the top of Capulin Mountain.

5) Socorro Caldera was created by the eruption of the Hells Mesa Tuff. The caldera is 32 million years old and roughly 12 to 30 miles in diameter. *FYI:* call the New Mexico Bureau of Mines and Mineral Resources, a division of New Mexico Tech; ask about their scenic trip series; 505-835-5420.

6) Mount Taylor (11,301 feet, an eroded composite volcano) might once have erupted much like Mt. St. Helens did in 1980.

7) Volcano Park, five tiny teats that were active during the Pleistocene, lies just west of Albuquerque off I-40,

Nature Trivia

☞ **The Enchanted Circle is 84 incredibly scenic miles looping Wheeler Peak, the highest mountain in the state. This is a U.S. Forest Service Scenic Byway.** *FYI:* **800-446-8117.**

☞ **Baker State Wildlife Area consists of 5,400 acres of wildlife habitat. In season, hunting is allowed. A good stop on the way to Capulin.** *FYI:* **15 miles northwest of the historic town of Cimarron.**

☞ **The Geology Museum at the University of New Mexico has exhibits of moon rocks, fossils, and minerals.** *FYI:* **Northrop Hall, University of New Mexico, Albuquerque; 505-277-4204.**

☞ **New Mexico Museum of Natural History features exhibits covering earth's history up to the twentieth century. A walk-through volcano is part of the permanent exhibit.** *FYI:* **1801 Mountain Road NW, Albuquerque; 505-841-8837.**

Ice Cave at El Malpais

Mine Time

DOD #1606 NM Records Center & Archives

Madrid tipple, Madrid circa 1940

For as long as humans have had the desire to remove minerals from the earth, geology has been an important part of New Mexico's economy. Native Americans mined chert and obsidian for tools, clays for pottery and decoration, coal for fuel, and salt and turquoise for trade.

Gold and silver eluded the early Spaniards, but later settlers found lead and turquoise near **Cerrillos** and copper at **Santa Rita**. Placer miners managed to mine millions of dollars' worth of gold from the **Ortiz Mountains** years before the California gold rush. Silver was discovered at **Magdalena** and **Georgetown** in the mid-1800s. In the last years of that century, copper and lead mining came into its own. Only a few decades or so ago, coal was mined at **Madrid**, and uranium was mined at **Grants**.

These days, the mines at Socorro, Red River Canyon, Elizabethtown, Magdalena, Madrid, Twining, Ute Creek, Cerrillos, and Hondo Canyon are closed, but coal is still mined in northwest New Mexico, and **Silver City** mines produce copper-silver-gold ores as well as manganese, zinc, and lead. Permian sedimentary rocks in eastern New Mexico produce limestone, gypsum, salt, and potash.

Rock Hound Heaven

Here's a first—a state park where they actually want you to take home some of the natural resources. **Rock Hound State Park**, located near Deming on the western slopes of the Little Florida (Flor-EYE-da) Mountains, covers 250 rock-filled acres.

The Florida Mountains take their name from "fluorite," which means minerals of different colors. True to their namesake, copious rocks of assorted shades and sizes abound for the enthusiastic hound. *FYI:* 14 miles south of Deming via NM11; camping and picnic facilities; 505-546-6182.

City of Rocks

This city of rocks was created when volcanic ash spewed from the earth's crust 30 million years ago. Streets, houses, towers, and temples were wind-carved, rain-worn, and sculpted by erosion. Ancient humans occupied this area. They made pottery, hunted, and buried their dead. Look for arrowheads and pottery shards.

City of Rocks State Park

Mark Nohl, courtesy NM Magazine

While some say the crosses carved by conquistadores on the rock face point the way to buried treasure, no one has discovered the code to date. *FYI:* 28 miles northwest of Deming via US180 and NM61; 505-536-2800.

Natural Attractions

☛ **Rock Hound Roundup** is sponsored by the Deming Gem & Mineral Society every March. The fun includes a gem and mineral show, guided rock trips, and auctions. *FYI:* Deming; 505-546-6209.

☛ **Carlsbad Caverns National Park** is also the location of the **Living Desert State Park**, where you can examine a variety of local rock types, including glittering white gypsum (left as the Permian sea dried up) used to edge the gardens. *FYI:* south of Carlsbad on US62/180; 505-785-2232.

☛ **Sunspot Solar Observatory** monitors the sun's activity with a vast telescope and other equipment. *FYI:* 18 miles south of Cloudcroft on Forest Rd. 64.

☛ **Natural History Museum** on campus at **Eastern New Mexico University** has wildlife exhibits that focus on bees and water life, among others. *FYI:* on campus, Portales; 505-562-2723.

☛ **Black Range Museum** (in the charming town of **Hillsboro**) has exhibits featuring mining artifacts that date back to the late nineteenth century. *FYI:* Main St.; 505-895-5652.

Down Below

If it weren't for bats, Carlsbad Caverns might still be an unknown cave system. The spectacle of hundreds of thousands of bats swirling out of the main cavern's natural entrance attracted the attention of curious and profit-minded settlers more than a century ago. Abundant bats meant abundant bat guano deposits. In the early part of the century, 100,000 tons of this natural fertilizer were excavated in the main cavern

Guano mining in the main cavern ended in the early 1920s but continued elsewhere in the park until the mid-1950s. In 1923, President Calvin Coolidge proclaimed Carlsbad Caverns a national monument. Up until that time, visitors entered via large buckets originally used by miners. Great bat flights occur from late April to late October, when the migratory Mexican freetail bats are roosting.

In the Big Room of Carlsbad Cavern, 830 feet below the earth's surface, sparkling columns (some reaching a 6-story height), draperies, flowstone, and other limestone formations boggle the mind with their seemingly infinite variation. These formations were created by an inland sea that covered the Southwest some 250 million years ago and by the wind and rain that followed.

This great underground chamber, one of the largest in the world, has space for 14 football fields. The U.S. Capitol building, complete with dome, could fit into one corner. There is an elevator, or you can walk down. The Luncheon Room looks like something out of *Star Trek*.

Carlsbad Caverns National Park covers 47,000 acres of spectacular desert and mountain scenery; it includes 75 known caves, only 2 of which are open for regularly scheduled tours: the main cavern and New Cave. *FYI:* 3225 National Parks Hwy; 505-785-2232.

Mark Nohl, courtesy NM Magazine

Entrance to Carlsbad Caverns

New Cave, 23 miles from Carlsbad's main cavern, can be toured during the summer season and, in the winter, only on weekends. The hike from the parking lot to New Cave is strenuous. The trail climbs 500 feet, the equivalent of a 50-story building, in a half mile. Guides point out ancient pictographs left by early Guadalupe Basket Makers and exotic formations such as Christmas Tree, a massive and crystalline version of its namesake. (This was a location for the film, *King Solomon's Mines*.) The tour takes about two hours, and people less than six years old are not permitted. Reservations required. You provide your own flashlight, canteen, and hiking footwear. *FYI:* 3225 National Parks Hwy; 505-785-2232. 🦇

The **Guadalupe Ridge** is one of the most amazing mountain ranges in the country. Attached to the Guadalupe Mountains to the south, the ridge was created by multitudinous marine plants and animals (including bryozoans, algae, corals, clams, snails, brachiopods) dating to the Permian. They created a great ancient reef—the Capitan Reef—much like the Great Barrier Reef of Australia. Most of the reef is underground, and what is visible was lifted by faulting. Carlsbad Cavern formed as a result of water dissolving passages through the limestone reef. *FYI:* southwest of Carlsbad Caverns National Park via US62/180.

The **Bat Flight Breakfast** (mid-August, annually) features thousands of bats in a pre-dawn entry to Carlsbad's main cavern. *FYI:* cave entrance, 5:00 to 7:00 a.m., Carlsbad Caverns National Park; 505-785-2232.

Mark Nohl, courtesy NM Magazine

The Guadalupe Mountains come alive with color in the fall.

BUILDING NEW MEXICO

Constructing History

Since the first multiunit "apartments" existed in New Mexico 900 years before Chicago's pioneer high-rises were conceived, it should come as no surprise that the Land of Enchantment is also the land of ancient architecture. Humans have been constructing fixed and lasting homes here for at least 1,500 years. Although the first pit houses (dating from A.D. 350) would have qualified as fixer-uppers, they were a vast improvement over no shelter at all. By the time buildings emerged aboveground, roughly A.D. 700, they were looking more hospitable, although the average real estate agent might have been reluctant to quote a list price. By A.D. 1100, the beginning of the Classic Pueblo period, Anasazi were living in towns and using masonry techniques that were the finest anywhere north of Mexico. And some of the great pueblos (beautiful in their design), constructed in the thirteenth century, are still in use today. With that kind of historical tradition, is it any wonder that New Mexico continues to inspire innovative architects to create unique structures?

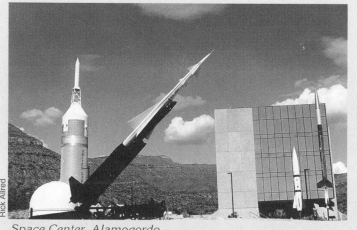

Space Center, Alamogordo

Charles E. Nolan Jr. & Associates created the starkly cubistic **International Space Hall of Fame** in 1976. Designed to evince the space age spirit, concrete monoliths brace five stories of reflective glass set against naked low-country desert.

FYI: Alamogordo; 505-437-2840 or 800-545-4021.

The Pottery House in Santa Fe was built from a design by Frank Lloyd Wright. Pottery House is privately owned.

Paolo Soleri Outdoor Amphitheater: Visionary architect Paolo Soleri and Pacheco & Graham created this provocative nuevo tech theater for the Institute of American Indian Arts in 1970. The audacious concrete forms were cast in dirt with earth-moving equipment and then hand finished. *FYI:* Santa Fe Indian School, 1502 Cerrillos Rd., Santa Fe; 505-989-6300.

The **Santa Fe Opera House** (1967) is a modern mix of open air, unpredictable weather, and flowing concrete forms. Designed by McHugh & Kidder, Burran, Wright, the novel structure incorporates technical breakthroughs necessary for an outdoor theatre of this caliber. Human artistry is set off by nature's scrim of blue mountains, starry nights, and frequent thundershowers. *FYI:* north of Santa Fe on US84/285.

In 1937, William Penhallow Henderson based the design of the **Wheelwright Museum** on a Navajo hogan. This earthy, elegant structure supports both traditional and innovative works by Native American artists. *FYI:* 704 Camino Lejo, Santa Fe; 505-982-4636.

Building Trivia

☞ **Pacheco & Graham designed the Immaculate Heart of Mary Church in Los Alamos in 1972. Skylights and whorling wood beams create a blend of traditional and modern styles.** *FYI:* **3700 Canyon Rd., Los Alamos.**
☞ **In a remote canyon of the Gila Wilderness Area, seven cliff caves house rock and mortar dwellings constructed by twelfth-century members of the Mogollon culture. Although the architecture may strike you as rudimentary, the builders were masters of the time** *FYI:* **505-536-9461.**

Dirty Business

The two most established methods of unbaked earth construction are adobe and pise. Adobe, an Arabic and Berber word introduced by Spaniards into the Americas, is a process in which earth, water, and straw are mixed and molded into bricks. The bricks are then sun-dried for several days before they are used to construct walls, domes, and vaults.

Pise, or rammed earth, first appeared in France in the sixteenth century. It's a method in which earth is compressed between parallel wooden plates that are eventually removed.

In the past, both adobe and pise methods were labor-intensive. These days, there are various adobe-making machines, and pneumatic rammers have replaced the bicep for molding pise. The methods may change, but the material—earth constitutes roughly 75 percent of the Earth's crust—remains the same.

The **Cristo Rey Church** was designed in 1940 by American architect John Gaw Meem. This Santa Fe structure is the largest modern public building made of raw earth in the United States. All 180,000 or so bricks were made on site. *FYI:* Canyon Rd., Santa Fe; 505-983-8528.

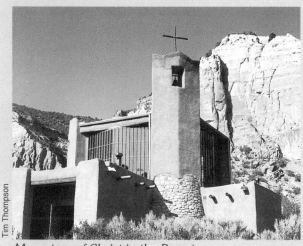

Tim Thompson

Monastery of Christ in the Desert

Monastery of Christ in the Desert, north of Abiquiu, was constructed around 1976 using the plans of architect George Yakashima. The contemporary design (made of unbaked earth) is well-suited for the rugged cliffs that surround the monastery. *FYI:* north of Abiquiu off US84 at the end of Forest Rd. 151.

Hassan Fathy is the Egyptian architect of this modern version of a traditional Islamic mosque at **Dar Al-Islam Educational Islamic Center**, which is located on 42 acres overlooking northern New Mexico's Chama River. This area was made famous by Georgia O'Keeffe's paintings, and it is the site of America's first Islamic village. Of special note are the Nubian vault and the dome. *FYI:* 505-685-4515.

Adobe Recipe

The term "adobe" can be applied to the building material, its final product, sun-cured bricks, and, even, to the local version of mud pie. Ancient Mesopotamians had mastered the technique of molding mud into bricks, and eventually Arabs taught it to

Patting adobes into forms, Madrid, 1935

the Spanish, who imported the method to Mexico, old and new. Native Americans had their own style of mud work, or "puddled adobe," in which bands of mud were poured in layers. Recently, modern architects in the Southwest have borrowed the Egyptian technique of creating vaults and domes without the use of a centring. ❧

Basic Adobe Bricks

This is a rough recipe for adobe bricks.

3 parts earth
1 part sand
a handful of straw and water

(Some adobe makers skip the sand because their soil already has lots of it naturally.) Stir until mixture is the consistency of thick cake batter. Pour into brick mold, known as adoberos, and let dry one to two days. Turn on end and dry for one week. Stack and let cure for one month.

Dirty Trivia

☞ **The average modern adobe brick measures 10" x 14" x 4" and weighs a good 35 pounds. Seventeenth-century bricks were longer and narrower (12" x 18" x 3").**

☞ **The Sagebrush Inn, Ranchos de Taos, dates back to 1930. Its pleasing design has helped create its long-lasting success.**

☞ **Taos Pueblo was founded circa 1250. The tiered dwellings still stand with elegant integrity.**

Old News

Palace of the Governors, Santa Fe, circa 1880

In New Mexico, old is not hard to find, but original is. Yes, the Palace of the Governors (constructed in 1610) may be considered the oldest continually operating official building in the United States. And, yes, Ácoma Pueblo is labeled the oldest continually occupied building in America. And, yes, the "oldest church" in Santa Fe is "old." But they've all been remodeled umpteen times; in many cases, foundations and portions of the early walls are the only remaining original parts. Ultimately, these continual building modifications attest to the flexibility of the state's building materials: mud, wood, metal, and, more recently, glass.

Colonial Combo

During almost 300 years of Spanish rule, life in New Mexico was so tough and existence so paltry, instead of converting resources to riches, the government concentrated on converting the native population to Christianity. Each friar packed a building kit, standard issue, which contained spade and ax, nails and hinges. With those tools, a new colony and new souls were to be forged.

New Mexico's colonial architecture is the almagamation of Native American and imported Spanish traditions. The basic structure—earth walls supporting a flat roof—was Indian. But the Spanish addition of adobe bricks and metal tools meant more rapid construction and efficiently worked timber for wooden doors, windows, and *portales* (porches).

Metal axes made it easier to fell great trees that could be used as roof beams, called *vigas*. The traditional Indian room (roughly 7 feet wide) could be expanded to 15 or 30 feet. This concept of open interior space is considered by some to be the greatest architectural contribution of the Spanish.

Colonial Churches and Missions

New Mexico has only thirty or so standing churches built before the nineteenth century, and roughly a dozen possess a credible colonial appearance. These listed below range from ruins to still-functioning churches.

☞ **Nuestra Señora de la Asunción de Zia:** This partially restored church contains a turn-of-the-century *retablo* (religious painting on wood). The original church was built in 1613 and destroyed in 1689 during fighting between Spanish and pueblo inhabitants. The pueblo converted to Catholicism, and another church was built in 1692. *FYI:* Zia Pueblo, 17 miles northwest of Bernalillo on NM44; 505-867-3304.

☞ **Nuestra Señora de Guadalupe de Zuñi:** A mission was established in 1629, but it was destroyed during the Pueblo Revolt. The church was rebuilt in 1699 and restored in the 1960s. Zuñi artist Alex Seowtewa restored interior murals from the eighteenth century. *FYI:* Zuñi Pueblo, west of Ramah on NM53; 505-782-4481.

☞ **Nuestra Señora de Purisma Concepción de Quarai:** When completed in 1629, this church had 60-foot-high and 6-foot-deep walls. Today, you can visit the ruins of the church and the convent. *FYI:* Salinas National Monument, Quarai; 505-847-2585.

☞ **San Esteban del Rey de Ácoma:** This lovely church was constructed between 1629 and 1641. All materials had to be hauled up the steep, narrow trail by hand or burro. Beams were 40 feet long and were transported from the Cebolleta Mountains more than 30 miles away. *FYI:* Ácoma Pueblo, 12 miles off I-40; 505-252-1139.

☞ **San Felipe:** This church dates to the eighteenth century, and it has changed very little. *FYI:* San Felipe Pueblo, off I-25, roughly 10 miles north of Bernalillo; 505-867-3381.

☞ **San Jose de Gracia Church:** This church received the President's Historic Preservation Award in 1992. The restoration was a remarkable community achievement. *FYI:* Las Trampas.

☞ **Holy Cross Church:** This lovely church was built in 1733. It's one of the largest Spanish colonial churches in the state. *FYI:* on the plaza, Santa Cruz.

☞ **Church of St. Francis of Assisi:** This unique example of Spanish Mission architecture was constructed in 1772. It's one of the most photographed churches in the United States. *FYI:* Ranchos de Taos, NM68; 505-758-2754.

Territorial Techniques

Courtesy Thompson Productions

Distinctive features of territorial architecture

When the Santa Fe Trail opened in the early 1820s, Yankee influence began to trickle westward from the East. But architecturally speaking, it took at least 25 years before change was noticeable. Technology (in addition to architectural style) was a contribution of the Americans. Run by the U.S. Army, the first sawmill—able to produce beams, boards, and posts—was established in Santa Fe in 1848. Mill assembly replaced handmade methods of construction, and doors and windows (the first glass windows were introduced by traders) reflected Greek Revival trends from the Midwest. Because New Mexico's Greek Revival style adapted itself to the frontier's economy and existing adobe architecture, it is called Territorial style.

The **Grand Hotel** was constructed in 1925 in Decorative Brick Commercial style (which is actually not very decorative). The exterior remains almost completely unaltered since the 1920s and 1930s. *FYI:* 306 West Coal Ave.

Harvey Hotel in Gallup: This building is on the State Register of Cultural Properties and dates to 1928. It should not be confused with Fred Harvey's legendary establishments. *FYI:* 408 West Coal Ave.

Railroads and Pueblo Deco

B y stagecoach, railroad, or Route 66, travelers have been rolling into **Gallup** for more than 100 years. The Blue Goose was the one-stop stagecoach service center before Gallup was a town. By 1881, a settlement grew up around the siding where David L. Gallup, railroad auditor and paymaster, gave company construction workers their hard-earned pay.

Gallup, located on the San Juan coal basin, quickly became a mining boomtown as the demand for coal to fuel locomotives increased. In addition to servicing the railroad, Gallup grew as an important trading center for commerce between Anglos and Native Americans. When **Route 66** (now 66 Avenue) was developed through the center of Gallup, highway travelers found rest and refreshment on their westward journey.

The **Gallup Historical Society** owns numerous historical buildings in town, and the organization conducts the Downtown Walking Tour during the annual **New Mexican Heritage Preservation Week** in May. Group tours can be arranged. *FYI:* P.O. Box 502, Gallup, NM 87301; 505-863-3841.

McNitt Collection, #6772 NM State Records Center & Archives

Well-known photographer Ben Wittick took this picture of Gallup, circa 1880

Las Vegas

801 THE FIDELITY BUILDING 803

Las Vegas rooftops

Tim Thompson

The valley of Las Vegas, "the meadows," has been a good place for humans to settle down for at least 10,000 years. Paleo-Indians, nomadic Plains Indians, and Spaniards have all pitched camp here.

In 1835, the Mexican government approved a land grant for 29 individuals, and the *Alcalde* (Administrative Justice) of San Miguel helped rough out the large plaza. By 1860, 1,000 people lived in Las Vegas.

In 1879, railroad tracks were completed east of the Gallinas River, one mile from the original plaza. Competition from other railroad towns, Clovis, Roswell, and Tucumcari, slowed growth in Las Vegas. But it was the depression in the 1930s that really dealt a blow to the local economy. During the last decade, Las Vegas has begun to revive. Many buildings have been restored: there are more than 900 on the historic register. East and West Las Vegas competed with each other until 1970, when they merged.

On Your Feet

Walking and driving tours sponsored by the Las Vegas Chamber of Commerce include some of the following buildings and areas. FYI: 505-425-8631 for a brochure.

Carnegie Park Historic District: This area boasts the finest examples of nineteenth-century landscape architecture in the state. Look for symmetry and lots of green space.

Bridge Street Historic District: Many buildings along this 800-foot-long section of Bridge Street date from between 1880 and 1910.

Old Town Residential District: This district provides a solid record of the move from Spanish/Mexican adobe to Anglo-American industrial age architecture, 1850-1915.

Plaza/Bridge Street Historic District: There are 14 buildings near and on the plaza that date back as far as 1879.

Stone Architecture of Las Vegas: These still-intact schools, churches, and residences were constructed between 1880 and 1898 and are representative of the Victorian Era.

The Mission Revival style **La Castaneda Hotel** was built in 1898-99 as part of Fred Harvey's amazing chain. Theodore Roosevelt and William Jennings Bryan stayed here. The lobby and dining room are both very much intact from the grand old days. *FYI:* 524 Railroad Ave., Las Vegas.

Castaneda Hotel, Las Vegas

Built in 1880, the **Plaza Hotel** was the place to see and be seen for local and visiting businessmen and ranchers. The Castaneda stole the show in 1899, but the Plaza is back in top form today. It even has its own ghost! *FYI:* 230 North Plaza, Las Vegas; 505-425-3591.

The **Aztec Main Street Historic District** includes buildings in a variety of architectural styles which are listed on the National Register of Historic Places and the New Mexico State Register of Cultural Properties. Aztec was mis-named for its "Aztec" ruins, which are actually Anasazi ruins. Oh, well. *FYI:* 505-334-9829

Plaza Hotel, Las Vegas

Mark Nohl, courtesy NM Magazine

The **Belen Harvey House**, an example of Mission style architecture, was constructed under the auspices of the Santa Fe Railway. Belen was settled by Spanish families in the mid-eighteenth century as part of a land grant. Belen is Spanish for Bethlehem. *FYI:* 104 N. 1st St., Belen.

Silver City's Historic District is the original site of Silver City, a mining town founded in 1870. Victorian homes, many made of local brick, are featured in this area, which is on the State and National registers. *FYI:* FYI: Silver City visitors information, 1103 N. Hudson; 505-538-3785.

Courtesy of Museum of New Mexico (Neg. #15264)

Archbishop Lamy's garden and carp pond, Santa Fe, circa 1880

Capital Gardens

Behind Garden Walls, sponsored by the Santa Fe Garden Club, lets you view Santa Fe's most beautiful gardens. There are four Tuesday tours each summer featuring four different homes. Transportation is by bus, and the cost is $25 per person (which goes toward city landscaping projects). Reservations must be made in advance, as these tours sell out quickly. *FYI:* Santa Fe Detours Hotline; 505-983-6565.

Do-It-Yourself Tour

1) El Zaguan: It was named "the passageway" because of the long walk that led between house and garden. This graceful hacienda dates to pre-1849 when prominent Santa Fean James L. Johnson purchased it as a rough, two-room adobe. Adolph Bandelier receives credit for the layout of the garden, where you can still see 100-year-old peony bushes. The trees are horse chestnuts, seeded by Johnson.

2) Sena Plaza: Although the property was originally part of the Arias de Quiros lands, it was given to the Sena family in 1844 by bequest. Coach house, servant's quarters, chicken house, and family residential quarters were all centered around the plaza. The building was restored in 1927 by the artist and architect, William Penhallow Henderson, who also designed the garden.

3) Randall Davey Audubon Center: The grounds are maintained by the Audubon Society, which now owns and operates the 135-acre historic site and nature sanctuary. The first sawmill in Territorial New Mexico was constructed here in 1847. Later, artist Randall Davey converted the sawmill into home and studio. *FYI:* 505-983-4609

La Plaza

Historically, *la plaza* was the center of all town activities—fiestas, executions, parades, town meetings, and promenades—in New Mexico for centuries. The social roots of the plaza can be traced to the Anasazi and to Mexico and Spain. Today, the state's plazas are still active places where you can spend an hour or a day. **Las Vegas, Santa Fe, Albuquerque, Taos**, and **Mesilla** all have historic plazas. **La Mesilla Plaza** is surrounded by brick streets dating to the 1800s, and the buildings are both Territorial and Pueblo style. *FYI:* Las Cruces visitors information, 505-524-8521 or 800-FIESTAS.

Mark Nohl, courtesy NM Magazine

One of New Mexico's many solar homes

The **New Deal** began in 1933. It was the moniker of President Franklin Roosevelt's domestic reform programs whose goal was to engineer the country's economic and social recovery. New Mexico's WPA buildings and projects are numerous. *FYI:* Community Foundation/ WPA Art Project, P.O. Box 149, Santa Fe, NM 87504-0149.

Southwest Regional Office, National Park Service Library; ineg.3WRO-58-29)

National Park Service Building under WPA construction

Going Solar

Sunshine isn't usually considered a building material, but it certainly plays a major role in designing contemporary homes and buildings in the sunbelt. Today, solar homes sprout up like energy-efficient weeds in and on New Mexico's valleys and hillsides.

The community of **Eldorado** (8 miles south of Santa Fe off US285) was one of the first in the nation to be planned around solar energy.

STATE OF THE ART

O ne of America's foremost artists, Georgia O'Keeffe lived much of her life in New Mexico. O'Keeffe was strongly influenced by the countryside surrounding her Abiquiu home.

Artful State

Although immigrant Easterners such as the founders of the illustrious art colonies of Taos and Santa Fe attracted international fame, a tradition of artistic excellence existed in the Southwest long before conquistadores noted there were no finer goldsmiths in the world than Pueblo Indian artisans. Today, art is still an important part of Pueblo life, the Navajo world view remains one in which individuals strive to live in beauty, and Apache traditions of artistic excellence in beadwork and basket weaving are very much alive.

New Mexico's Hispanic artists, too, have excelled in traditional art forms—wood carving, tinwork, furniture making, painting, weaving, sculpting—and taken them to new levels of mastery.

Taos Talent

The Taos Society of Artists was founded in 1912 but had its first meeting in 1915 at the home of Dr. T. P. Martin (the present-day Taos Inn). Co-founder Ernest Blumenschein, Henry Sharp, Bert Phillips, Oscar Berninghaus, Herbert Dunton, and Irving Couse were the six artists present. The purpose of the organization was to "develop a high standard of art among its members and to aid in the diffusion of taste for art in general." Today, the co-founder's home is the **Ernest Blumenschein Memorial Home and Art Museum**. *FYI:* 2 blocks west of the plaza on Ledoux St., Taos; 505-758-0505.

The Institute of American Indian Arts Museum, Santa Fe, houses the National Collection of Contemporary Indian Art. This is the Smithsonian for Native Americans, and the permanent collection includes the work of such prominent artists as Earl Biss, T. C. Cannon, Josephine Wapp, Darren Vigil Gray, Fritz Scholder, Doug Hyde, Allan Houser, Charles Loloma, and Kevin Red Star. *FYI:* 108 Cathedral Pl., Santa Fe; 505-988-6211.

Mabel Dodge Luhan (1879-1962)

Mabel Dodge Luhan was a wealthy and headstrong Bostonian, a mover and shaker in art and literary circles, who transplanted herself to Taos in the 1920s and married her fourth husband, Tony Luhan, a Pueblo Indian. Mabel Dodge Luhan imported an amazing assortment of famous people to Taos, including D. H. Lawrence (her best-known protégé) and Frida Kahlo. One of Mabel's guest lists might have included Willa Cather, Thomas Wolfe, Aldous Huxley, and Georgia O'Keeffe. *FYI:* Mabel Dodge Luhan's Taos home is privately owned and operated as a learning resource center; 505-758-9456.

E. Boyd Collection # 35959, NM State Records Center & Archives

Mabel Dodge Luhan (left) with Frida Lawrence and Dorothy Brett

Modern Native American artists, such as the late **Popovi Da** and **Maria Montoya Martinez**, gained international fame for their mastery of traditional ceramic techniques and their innovative expression. Today, the award-winning work of some of New Mexico's native artists can be admired at Santa Fe's annual **Indian Market** (August). *FYI:* Southwestern Association on Indian Affairs; 505-983-5220.

DOD #37364 NM State Records Center & Archives

Famous potter Maria Montoya Martinez (center) at work circa 1940

Environmental Art

Walter de Maria's environmental art installation, the **Lightning Field**, offers visitors an electric, one-of-a-kind, overnight experience. Four hundred gleaming steel spires are set in a rectangular grid that measures one mile by 3,300 feet. Artist De Maria searched five years and six western states to find ideal conditions for his environmental art installation. His requirements were isolation, flat space, and high lightning activity. This 5 3/4-section parcel, at a high desert elevation of 7,200 feet, provides a starkly beautiful setting from which to experience the Lightning Field.

A gray and weathered cabin, built in the 1930s, lodges visitors to the Field. Furnishings are rustic: a long, handcrafted dining table, a wood stove, and rough hewn cabinets. Dinner is provided, but you cook.

Some say the Lightning Field is a power spot; this can dazzle even the most jaded. *FYI:* The Lightning Field, Two Wind NW, Albuquerque, NM 87120; 505-898-5602.

In 1990, 7,100 acres northwest of Albuquerque were designated as **Petroglyph National Monument**. You can explore the main park—which includes five extinct volcanoes, numerous Native American shrines, and more than 15,000 petroglyphs—on any of three self-guided trails. Snakes, birds, masked figures, and lightning patterns decorate the ancient rock. Prehistoric people left behind no written language, but these pictures really are worth any number of words. *FYI:* 505-766-8375 or 839-4429.

Portales resident Bill Dalley is known as the **"Windmill Man"** because he has restored sixty windmills that now rise from his property. For Dalley, they symbolize New Mexico's pioneer spirit. *FYI:* Portales visitors information; 505-356-8541.

Art in Public

Cruising San Mateo I (commonly called "Chevy on a Stick") is part of the city of Albuquerque's Public Art Program dedicated to "enhancing the urban environment." This ceramic tile, steel, and concrete sculpture by Barbara Grygutis is located on San Mateo and Gibson SE.

Cruising San Mateo I

There are more than 150 artworks in the program, mostly by New Mexico's artists. While you're cruising, check out Gary Mercer's 1991 steel sculpture, **Running Horses**, at the Albuquerque International Airport, and Glenna Goodacre's **Sidewalk Society**, a 1991 bronze sculpture at 3rd St. and Tijeras NW. 🐎

Art Trivia

1) Cochiti artists are renowned for their _____-making skills.
a) drum b) love c) bread

2) Taos Pueblo has a reputation for producing _____ made from wood.
a) Frisbees b) flutes c) fiddles

3) Jewelry bearing the stamp "reservation made" may come from a location in _____ known as Reservation.
a) Japan b) New Mexico
c) Germany

4) _____ is a tribal tradition (and almost an art) that has brought national acclaim to Jémez Pueblo.
a) singing b) dancing
c) running

Answers: 1) a 2) b 3) a 4) c

The Art of Trivia

☞ **The Kuaua Pueblo ruin at Coronado State Monument and Park was partially restored in 1936 by a WPA project. Its kiva frescoes depict Pueblo gods and their fifteenth-century worshipers.** *FYI:* 505-867-5589.

☞ **Shakespeare in the Park, Santa Fe, is free every August and September.** *FYI:* 505-984-6760 or 800-777-CITY.

☞ **The traditional Santa Fe Powwow, each May at the Downs at Santa Fe, offers you the chance to see dances and purchase art, all out of doors.** *FYI:* **Southwestern Association on Indian Affairs Inc.;** 505-983-5220.

☞ **At Shidoni Foundry and Galleries in Tesuque (near Santa Fe), you can stroll through the outdoor sculpture garden or the gallery.** *FYI:* 505-988-8001.

ANOTHER VICTIM OF SANTA FE STYLE

Jerry Milord's spoof on Santa Fe

Capital Art

It's been called the art capital of the Southwest, and although Santa Fe's often-printed claim of "third-largest art market in the country" is unproven, the town's Yellow Pages do boast at least 250 listings under the heading of "Art Galleries, Dealers, & Consultants." Since the official population of the city proper is 48,899, that computes to one gallery per 195 people. If you plan to tour Santa Fe's galleries, pack provisions for several days. And be careful, or you might become another victim of Santa Fe Style.

Jerry Milord's poster, **Another Victim of Santa Fe Style**, made the Smithsonian Institution's "American Encounters" exhibit in 1992. According to Harold Closter, project manager for the exhibit, the poster represents the interaction between tourists and the indigenous cultures of Santa Fe. *FYI:* 505-982-2531.

Capital Music

In addition to the Santa Fe Opera, the Chamber Music Festival, the Orchestra of Santa Fe, and the Desert Chorale, there's the **Annual Santa Fe Banjo and Fiddle Contest**, which began in 1974 and grew to its present two-day competition of bluegrass and old-time music. Every Labor Day weekend, there are workshops, a jam session, and a folk dance, in addition to the contest. The event is sponsored by the Southwest Traditional & Bluegrass Music Association. *FYI:* Banjo and Fiddle Contest, Santa Fe Rodeo Grounds, Rt. 7, Box 115-BK, Santa Fe, NM 87505; 505-984-6760 or 800-777-CITY.

Tommy S. Macaione (1907-1992)

Up until his death on October 26, 1992, artist Tommy Macaione—complete with paintbrush and easel—was a Santa Fe landmark seen on street corners all over town. Macaione was a true character. Although he gained recognition as a serious painter, he didn't rest on his laurels. Here was a man who announced his presidential candidacy in 1988 to promote the "Mutual Happiness Society." A year later he declared himself a write-in candidate for state governor. He once threatened to shoot Santa Fe's mayor, and he was known to tip a taxi driver fifty bucks.

Perhaps Tommy's old friend, journalist Lew Thompson, summed up Macaione best: "Everyone loved Tommy. He was Santa Claus to little children. He didn't have to go through costuming or make-up. He was a clown, a fool, a prophet, and a statesman."

Tim Thompson

Internationally famous flamenco artist **Maria Benitez** and her troupe, Estampa Flamenca, perform in Santa Fe every summer. *FYI:* 505-984-6760 or 800-777-CITY.

Marguerite Meier and friends organized Santa Fe's first annual **shrine show** in 1986. Now, the grass-roots shrine show is one of the city's favorite events, and more than 75 shrines are on view at various galleries and on street corners. This is a refreshing change from commercial art. *FYI:* 505-984-6760 or 800-777-CITY.

Roadside Art Stop

In the desert, you never know when you'll spy the elusive roadrunner or coyote whizzing across the road. So it is with "Art" in New Mexico. Just when you think you're in the middle of aesthetic nowhere, you turn the corner and collide with a gallery offering exotica, erotica, or environmental esoterica. Whether you're passing through Thoreau (pronounced "through"), on your way to Taos, or Madrid (accent on the first syllable), or just plain nowhere, an unscheduled stop may yield aesthetic treasures.

Studio Tours & Art Shows

To See Where the Artists Roam

Many towns offer studio tour weekends when local artists and artisans open their doors to the public. This is a great way to get to know the people and their work. It's also a way to see a community from the inside.

Taos: Taos Fall Arts Festival is the place to browse and buy arts and crafts by locals. *FYI:* Taos Chamber of Commerce; 505-758-3873 or 800-732-8267.

Dixon: Artists and craftsmen here host open studios early each November. The event is sponsored by the Dixon Arts Association. *FYI:* Hwy 68 between Española and Taos; 505-753-2831.

Madrid: Christmas in Madrid features gallery open houses in early December. Of course, stores are open year-round. *FYI:* Hwy 14 south of Santa Fe.

Galisteo: Potters and painters participate in this studio tour, held each fall. The town is charming. *FYI:* Hwy 41, southwest of Santa Fe; 505-984-6760 or 800-777-CITY.

Deming: Work is on display each June at the Deming Arts and Crafts Fair. *FYI:* 505-546-2674.

Mark Nohl, courtesy NM Magazine

Art and craft galleries and studios are numerous in historic Madrid

Music to Your Ears

What the opera is to Santa Fe, so the **ball park** is to nearby **Madrid**. On most summer Sundays there's live music—jazz, blues, or chamber—beginning in the mid-afternoon. Pack a cooler and picnic in the shade of the ball park pavilion, or bring your own umbrella and spread a blanket.

Madrid has survived many incarnations. Used to be, in the boomtown days of coal mining in the late 1800s, you could rent a house for $2 a month. In the 1950s, Madrid earned the right to call itself a ghost town, but a decade later, the "flower children" moved in. And one day in 1974, the Huber family, which had been trying to sell Madrid for years, set up the ultimate yard sale: all yards (and the houses on them) were on sale to the highest bidder. *FYI:* 20 miles south of Santa Fe on State Route 22.

WPA Art

For almost ten years, New Mexico's artists toiled and created under the direction of the Public Works of Art Project (PWAP), the Federal Art Projects (FAP), the Treasury Relief Art Project (TRAP), and of course, the Works Projects Administration (WPA). Under PWAP, FAP, TRAP, and WPA, hundreds of artworks in the state were produced between 1933 and 1943. *FYI:* Community Foundation/ WPA Art Project, P.O. Box 149, Santa Fe, NM 87504-0149.

Russel Vernon Hunter (1900-1955)

Government muralist Russell Vernon Hunter painted "The Last Frontier" for the De Baca County Courthouse in 1934. The work was completed at his studio (a rented store) in Texico. It was transported to Fort Sumner by truck and glued to the wall. From 1934 to 1942, Hunter served as director of the state's largest federal art program under the WPA.

Literary New Mexico

Travel east of US54 close to the old Three Rivers service station just north of Tularosa and bump across the rusty tracks of the Southern Pacific toward the foothills of the Sierra Blanca, and you may happen on one of Tony Hillerman's magic places. This high ridge, overlooking the Tularosa Basin, White Sands, and New Mexico's badlands, has worked its creative magic ever since Stone Age hunters told their tales in stone.

Tony Hillerman (b. 1925)

Tony Hillerman, a former executive editor of the *New Mexican* now living in Albuquerque, is well known for mystery novels that are filled with the mysticism of Navajo culture. His award-winning books include *A Thief of Time* and the best-seller *Skinwalker*.

D. H. Lawrence (1885-1930)

D. H. Lawrence, born in England, established his Taos residence at the urging of social and literary doyenne Mabel Dodge Luhan. While his stay was brief—the fall and winter of 1922-23 and the spring and summer of 1925—it established Lawrence as one of the state's literary legends. Lawrence's ashes are said to be enshrined on Lobo Mountain, 15 miles north of Taos, in San Cristobal. But, according to at least one version of Lawrence lore, the writer's ashes may have been tossed out with the trash at the La Fonda Hotel after inebriated couriers stopped for refreshment and left their precious cargo behind. If you believe that tale, the ashes in the shrine are fireplace sweepings.

Farrar Collection #36634 NM State Records Center & Archives

New Mexico authors date back to 1610 when Gaspar Perez de Villagra wrote his epic poem, "Historia del Nuevo Méjico." The Land of Enchantment is still writer's country, and its blue mesas, salty arroyos, and great plains belong to paper as well as canvas. Some of the state's most celebrated authors include John Nichols and Leslie Marmon Silko.

Jimmy Santiago Baca (b. 1952)

Poet Jimmy Santiago Baca was born in Santa Fe and spent much of his youth in Albuquerque's South Valley. Orphaned as a child, by the time he was a teenager he had run-ins with the police and ultimately ended up in prison, where he began to read and write. His books include *Black Mesa Poems* (New Directions, 1989), *Martin and Meditations on the South Valley* (New Directions, 1987), and a book of personal essays, *Working in the Dark* (Red Crane Books, 1992). Baca wrote the screenplay for, acted in, and is the exective producer of the 1993 film *Blood In, Blood Out.*

Michael O Shaughnessy, Red Crane Books

Simon Ortiz (b. 1941)

Simon Ortiz has a reputation as one of the most influential Native American poets of our time. He is the author of many books including *From Sand Creek* (winner of the Pushcart Prize in 1982) and *Fightin': New and Collected Stories.* Ortiz is an Ácoma Pueblo Indian. He served in the U.S. Army before graduating from the University of New Mexico and the University of Iowa. His book, *Fight Back: For the Sake of the People, For the Sake of the Land,* is an indictment of New Mexico's uranium industry. His latest book is *Woven Stone.*

Literary Quiz

Who wrote...? about an "extinct civilization, hidden away in this inaccessible mesa for centuries, preserved like a fly in amber, guarded by the cliffs and the river and the desert"?

—Willa Cather, in "Tom Outland's Story" from the novel, *The Professor's House*

Who wrote...? "Never shall I forget the Christmas dances at Taos, twilight, snow, the darkness coming over the great wintry mountains and the lonely pueblo, then suddenly, again, like dark calling to dark, the deep Indian cluster-singing around the drum, wild and awful, suddenly arousing on the last dusk as the procession starts."

—D. H. Lawrence

Who wrote...? about "a drunk man dancing alone, raising little clouds of dust in the sunlight. We'll just get some mutton at the trading post and cook it under the trees here. Let's make tortillas, too. And pop—regular Pepsi and Diet Pepsi for those on diets (as if it would help after eating ribs!)."

—Navajo poet Luci Tapahonso

Who wrote...? an unprecedented work with Hopi elders which revealed their long-kept secrets of the world and its creation? He lived as a boy on the Navajo Reservation and spent most of his life in the Southwest.

—Frank Waters, *The Book of Hopi*

Who wrote...? *House Made of Dawn*? He grew up on reservations in the Southwest, is a member of the Kiowa tribe, and was educated at Stanford University.

—N. Scott Momaday

On location at Ácoma Pueblo, 1929

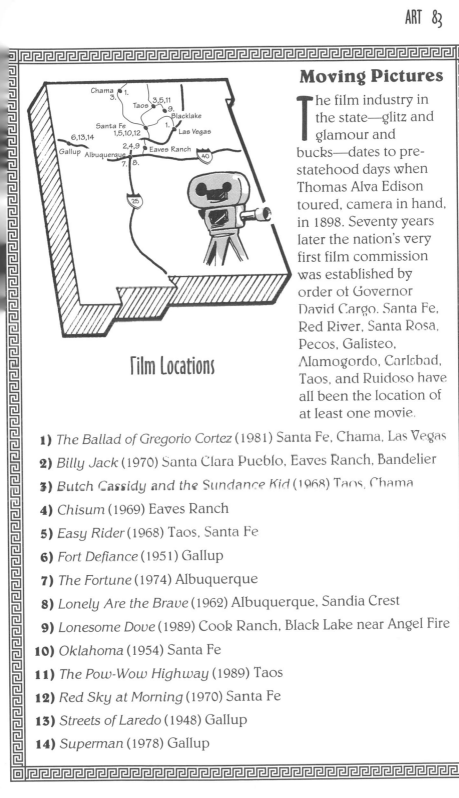

Film Locations

Moving Pictures

The film industry in the state—glitz and glamour and bucks—dates to pre-statehood days when Thomas Alva Edison toured, camera in hand, in 1898. Seventy years later the nation's very first film commission was established by order of Governor David Cargo. Santa Fe, Red River, Santa Rosa, Pecos, Galisteo, Alamogordo, Carlsbad, Taos, and Ruidoso have all been the location of at least one movie.

1) *The Ballad of Gregorio Cortez* (1981) Santa Fe, Chama, Las Vegas

2) *Billy Jack* (1970) Santa Clara Pueblo, Eaves Ranch, Bandelier

3) *Butch Cassidy and the Sundance Kid* (1968) Taos, Chama

4) *Chisum* (1969) Eaves Ranch

5) *Easy Rider* (1968) Taos, Santa Fe

6) *Fort Defiance* (1951) Gallup

7) *The Fortune* (1974) Albuquerque

8) *Lonely Are the Brave* (1962) Albuquerque, Sandia Crest

9) *Lonesome Dove* (1989) Cook Ranch, Black Lake near Angel Fire

10) *Oklahoma* (1954) Santa Fe

11) *The Pow-Wow Highway* (1989) Taos

12) *Red Sky at Morning* (1970) Santa Fe

13) *Streets of Laredo* (1948) Gallup

14) *Superman* (1978) Gallup

THE SPORTING LIFE

Re-creating Recreation

Back in the days when most sunups to sundowns were spent hunting, digging, hauling, and planting, New Mexicans knew how to enjoy themselves when the work was finished. Dancers twirled and musicians fiddled through the night until the next sunrise, harvest celebrations were feasts that lasted for several days, and roundups turned into family reunions.

New Mexicans still know how to have fun—only now there's more time and more to choose from. Feast days and fiestas are still annual events, but hot-air ballooning, mountain biking, hang gliding, rock climbing, and even llama backpacking are part of the pleasure, too.

The **Fiesta del Valle de Española** is a three-day annual event that includes an Olympic-style torch-run ceremony, a candlelight procession, fireworks, a children's parade, a grand ball, canoe races, and a mariachi Mass. Each July, people from the town of Española and the surrounding valley come together to celebrate the old way. *FYI:* Española visitors' information; 505-753-2831.

On Your Feet

New Mexico's **Bureau of Land Management** oversees about 13 million acres of public land, much of which offers a full range of recreational opportunities. In the **Wild Rivers Recreation Area** (roughly 35 miles north of Taos), hikers, campers, and picnickers can explore the Red and Rio Grande scenic rivers. *FYI:* Taos Resource Area, Montevideo Plaza, 224 Cruz Alta Rd., Taos, NM 87571; 505-758-8851.

Explore 462 acres of ancient volcanic lava flow at **Valley of Fires Recreation Area** (about 5 miles west of Carrizozo) for day and night use. *FYI:* Roswell Resource Area, 5th and Richardson, Roswell, NM 88201; 505-624-1790.

Bureau of Land Management wilderness areas can be explored at the **Bisti and De-Na-Zin**. FYI: Farmington Resource Area, 1235 La Plata Highway, Farmington, NM 87401. The **West Malpais** and **Cebolla** areas also keep visitors on their toes. *FYI:* El Malpais Visitor Information Center, 620 E. Santa Fe, Grants, NM 87020; 505-285-5406.

Llamas, anyone?

If your own two feet are over-worked, you might entertain the thought of letting a four-legged member of the Camelid family carry your burden. These guys are strong and surefooted, and they won't talk your ear off. Indigenous to the South American Andes, llamas have been beasts of burden for more than 3,500 years. Although North American llamas might seem a bit trendy, fossil records show that their ancestors traversed New Mexico, Colorado, Arizona, and Utah very long ago. They're back, they're terrific packers, and yes, they do spit—but only when under great duress. You might try a camel drop, an artist's retreat, or a family trip. *FYI:* Sangre de Cristo Wilderness Adventures, a member of Worldwide Outfitter and Guide Association, the Wilderness Society, and the Rocky Mountain Llama Association, 633 N. Star Route, Questa, NM 87556.

More Ways to Recreate

☞ Hunters can go to the source by contacting the **New Mexico Council of Outfitters and Guides**—these are independent guides from all four corners of the state—for a brochure. *FYI:* 160 Washington SE, #75, Albuquerque, NM 87108; 505-243-4461.

☞ The **Quebradas** is a 24-mile scenic Bureau of Land Management Back Country Byway where you can gaze at pastel cliffs, formations, and badlands. *FYI:* 5 miles east of I-25 and 5 miles north of Socorro.

Courtesy of Sangre de Cristo Wilderness Adventures

Llamas and friend

North
Cascades

Roger's Pass
Bridgers

Wellsvilles

Goshutes

Marin
Bad Lands

Grand Canyon

Sandias
Manzanos

**Raptor
Migration
Flyways and
Project Sites**

Veracruz

Life List

Birders can add sandhill cranes, snow geese, and other species of waterfo and shorebirds to their l list after a winter stop at **Bitter Lake National Wildlife Refuge** (locate along the Pecos River or the southeastern plains). The refuge's **Salt Creek Wilderness** area is oper to the public. *FYI:* Box 7 Roswell, NM 88201; 505-622-6755.

The 57,200 acres of **Bosque del Apache National Wildlife Refuge** (93 miles south o Albuquerque along the Rio Grande) host sandhill cranes, snow geese, Canadian geese, and a variety of duck species. This is one of the state's special attractions. *FYI:* P.O. Box 1246, Socorro, NM 87801; 505-835-1828.

HawkWatch International Inc., an Albuquerque-based research group, has been monitoring bird of prey migration routes in the state for more than five years. Their annual counts of raptors migrating over the Manzano Mountains southeast of Albuquerque confirm that bird numbers seem to be on the increase. *FYI:* 505-255-7622.

The **Las Vegas National Wildlife Refuge** is the place to spot migrating wintering waterfowl. If you're lucky, you may see a bald eagle or a falcon passing through. *FYI:* Rt. 1, Box 399, Las Vegas NM 87701; 505-425-3581.

Grulla National Wildlife Refuge (Roosevelt County near Arch) is a winter roosting area for lesser sandhill cranes. *FYI:* P.O. Box 549, Muleshoe, TX 79347; (806) 946-3341.

No doubt about it, the **Kodak Albuquerque International Balloon Fiesta** is one of the largest air shows in the world, with as many as 500 participants and thousands of spectators. Festivities include the opening day parade, air shows, a precision parachute team, marching bands, souvenirs, lots to eat, and the lovely evening balloon glow. *FYI:* Balloon Park, Albuquerque; 505-821-1000.

Mark Nohl, courtesy NM Magazine

Each year in mid-May, the residents of Lamy and friends are flying high at the **Lamy Kite Festival**. Contests, food, and prizes abound at this celebration of the art and sport of kite flying. The public is welcome; bring a picnic. *FYI:* Hwy 285 south of Santa Fe; (Legal Tender) 505-982-8425.

Mark Nohl, courtesy NM Magazine

Rafting the Taos Box, Rio Grande River

Desert Water

Whether you're twelve or twelve-times-six, there's no excuse not to try white-water rafting on the world-famous **Rio Grande Wild and Scenic River** if the season is right. Spring and early summer promise the highest and wildest water through "The Box," when river rafts and kayaks ricochet off rapids like Hangman, Powerline, and Ski Jump. Slow-float trips are available, also, for those who prefer travel in the mellow lane. If you decide to try this, reputable companies will supply you with qualified guides and excellent equipment. The Chama River is also officially designated "Wild and Scenic," and it's a challenging run for rafters and kayakers. *FYI:* The BLM in Taos has a complete list of statewide outfitters; 505-758-8851.

Skeez It

If you prefer your water frozen, winter sports in New Mexico include skiing, sledding, and snow boarding. Great runs can be made at any of New Mexico's eight downhill ski areas: **Santa Fe**, **Angel Fire**, **Red River**, **Sandia Peak**, **Sipapu**, **Ski Apache**, **Pajarito**, and **Taos Ski Valley**. Snow boards, a kind of winterized skateboard, are becoming increasingly popular on winter slopes. There's also great cross-country skiing at **Enchanted Forest** ski area and on forest roads and hiking trails in New Mexico's national forests. Forest ranger stations provide weekly recommendations.

Fly fishing in the Rio Grande

Go Fish

New Mexico's rivers are known for their excellent **fly fishing**. Fall is the loveliest time to cast over the waters of the **Pecos**, **Rio Grande**, or **Chama rivers**. The **San Juan River** at Navajo Lake is internationally renowned for its superb year-round fly fishing. On several miles of this river there is a special limit of one trout only over 20 inches. Those who fish with lures or bait can catch crappie, walleye, and salmon at **Eagle Nest**, **Ute**, and **Conchas lakes**. *FYI:* Department of Game and Fish; 505-827-7911.

Wet Trivia

☛ **You can also take the path of least resistance: a relaxing soak in the outdoor tubs of Ten Thousand Waves above Santa Fe.** *FYI:* **Ski Basin Rd., Santa Fe. Reservations; 505-982-9304. Or ease into an old-fashioned mineral bath at Ojo Caliente, an hour north of Santa Fe.**

☛ **Take in 13 miles of Wild Rivers by car on this scenic Back Country Byway that begins in the Rio Grande Valley (roughly 28 miles north of Taos).** *FYI:* **New Mexico State Office, 120 S. Federal Pl., Santa Fe, NM 87504; 505-988-6000.**

Hot-dog **windsurfers** do their thing on Morgan Lake, a man-made cooling pond (near Four Corners power plant) in winter months only (summer water is too hot). Other windsurfing and boating lakes include Cochiti (good for beginners), Storrie (intermediate/advanced), and Eagle Nest. Peak winds blow in spring and fall. *FYI:* Santa Fe Windsurfing info, classes, and equipment), 505-473-7900; or dial City Line, 505-843-6060, ext. SURF.

Strong Stuff

For those who like their sporting activities in grueling fours, the **Mount Taylor Winter Quadrathlon** might do. First there's biking: entrants gain more than 1,800 feet in 13 miles, and there's an 800-foot gain in the last 2 miles. Survive that, and you get to run. This time the gain is a mere 1,200 feet in more than 5 miles, with over half the gain in the last 2 miles. Ah, now there's skiing. Gain 1,200 feet in 2 miles, and the name of Heartbreak Hill gives you a good idea of what the last stretch is like. Finally, strap on your snowshoes and gain 600-plus feet in 1 mile (that's 100 feet the first 1/2 mile and 500 feet the last 1/2 mile). It's been called one of the "top multi-sports events in the country." *FYI:* Mount Taylor Winter Quadrathlon, P.O. Box 85, Grants, NM 87020; 505-285-6969.

Mark Nohl, courtesy NM Magazine

Horse racing at the Santa Fe Downs

Fast Track

It has been six decades since New Mexico's Legislature voted to approve pari-mutuel activity on the state's race-tracks. The Land of Enchantment is no longer a bush-track circuit; there are five full-blown tracks conducting seven meets each year. It all adds up to a very lucrative $250 million year-round industry. *FYI:* Department of Tourism for complete track data; 800-235-3247 or (locally) 827-0291.

☞ **Downs at Santa Fe:** June through Labor Day; 505-471-3311.
☞ **Downs at Albuquerque:** Roughly $3 million in purses; mid-January through April; 505-262-1188.
☞ **Ruidoso Downs:** Some of the best quarter horse racing in the country; 505-378-4431.
☞ **Sunland Park:** Heavy quarter horse lineup, October through May; 505-589-1131.
☞ **San Juan Downs:** The state's newest racetrack, opens in late April and runs through Labor Day.
☞ **New Mexico State Fair:** The state's oldest and shortest racing meet, also the richest; the purse structure is greater than $500,000; 17 consecutive days in September, then three days a week through October.

Racing Trivia Quiz

) Which track features 18 stakes races, 10 for thoroughbreds, 6 for quarter horses, and 2 for appaloosas?
   a) Upson Downs b) Downs at Chupadero c) State Fair

2) The _____ is New Mexico's 13-race, $200,000 showcase for Land of Enchantment-bred quarter horses and thoroughbreds. This is growing in popularity each year.
   a) Lineage b) Cochiti Triathalon c) Great American Duck Races

3) On which day is the world's richest quarter horse race held at Ruidoso Downs?
   a) Christmas Day b) Labor Day c) Mother's Day d) Midday

Answers: 1) c 2) a 3) b

If your luck's not holding at the horse races, try the **Great American Duck Races** held in Deming each year in late August. Besides quacky races, festivities include hot-air balloon races, dances, a tortilla toss, a flea market, and assorted booths. This is a popular one. *FYI:* 505-546-2674.

Rodeo Fever

New Mexico is rodeo land, at the heart of the nation's professional rodeo circuit. Lovington boasts the state's largest purse for professional competition: $28,500. Statewide, there are more than 10 pro rodeos. Local amateur competitions are too numerous to count, but contact the chamber of commerce in the area you plan to visit for information. For a complete listing of rodeos and events, contact the **Professional Rodeo Cowboys Association**: 719-593-8840.

Santa Fe Rodeo

Mark Nohl, courtesy NM Magazine

Pro Rodeo Schedule

Santa Fe	July
Grants	July
Raton	June
Tucumcari	June
Gallup	August
Lovington	August
Roswell	Sept.
Silver City	May
Clovis	June
Mountainair	June

Mark Nohl, courtesy NM Magazine

The Klansman, Carlsbad Caverns National Park

Straight Up, Deep Down

For those who prefer to get their exercise belowground, New Mexico's public lands offer equal opportunities. Many caves are located in the southwestern area of the state, and a free-use permit must be obtained before you venture into gated caves. When you find a cave that shows signs of bat activity, do not enter; bats are highly endangered, very beneficial critters. *FYI:* Carlsbad Resource Area, 101 E. Mermod, Carlsbad, NM 88220, 505-887-6544; or Roswell Resource Center, 5th and Richardson, Roswell, NM 88201, 505-624-1790.

The **Potrillo Cliffs**, near White Rock, offer all levels of climbers a variety of breathtaking choices: sheer walls, overhanging cliffs, and extremely steep paths. The canyon extends from the southern hip of White Rock down to the Rio Grande. The view from the top stretches out to Chino Mesa, the Ortiz Mountains, the Rio Grande Valley, and the Manzano and Sandia mountains. Rock climbing should only be attempted by professionals or with professional guidance. *FYI:* for info on mountaineering and ice climbing and the Los Alamos Mountaineer Club, call Trail Bound Sports, Los Alamos; 505-662-3000.

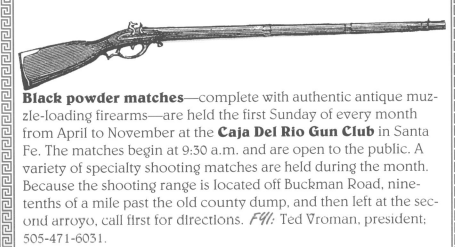

Black powder matches—complete with authentic antique muzzle-loading firearms—are held the first Sunday of every month from April to November at the **Caja Del Rio Gun Club** in Santa Fe. The matches begin at 9:30 a.m. and are open to the public. A variety of specialty shooting matches are held during the month. Because the shooting range is located off Buckman Road, nine-tenths of a mile past the old county dump, and then left at the second arroyo, call first for directions. *FYI:* Ted Vroman, president; 505-471-6031.

The **Blue Hole**, an old and deep artesian well near Santa Rosa, rates in the top ten for freshwater dives in the nation. The Blue Hole is more than 100 feet deep, and the clear water allows great visibility. Even though New Mexico may seem like a thirsty state, there are hundreds (maybe even thousands) of certified divers in Santa Fe alone. Santa Fe is also the base of the National Park Service's **Submerged Cultural Resources Unit**. NPS divers and diving archaeologists work underwater in all of the nation's parks. *FYI:* Inner Vision Divers, Santa Fe; 505-988-6750.

THE SPIRIT OF NEW MEXICO

Tim Thompson

An aikido lesson by the sensei

The Healing Spirit

Long before the first Europeans arrived in the Southwest, Native Americans were using herbs, minerals, and sacred ceremonies to heal the sick. Spanish *curanderas* (healers) brought their own cures from the Old World and Mexico, many of which are still in use. The healing tradition continues in New Mexico, and aura balancing, arsenic baths, past-life regression therapy, and ceremonial sweats are a few of the ways residents and visitors say *a santé*.

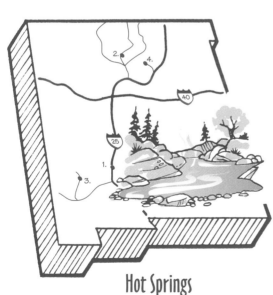

Hot Springs

Healthy Soaks

Anasazi farmers, conquistadores, outlaws, and nuclear physicists have all soaked in the healing mineral springs surrounding Santa Fe. Ojo Caliente offers arsenic and iron water, the old Montezuma hot springs near Las Vegas once soothed the aches and pains of Billy the Kid, and according to local folklore, Juan Vásquez de Coronado bathed in the springs at Jémez.

1) Geronimo's Spring:
These mineral waters were credited with healing power

long before the first Europeans arrived in New Mexico. Legend has it that Geronimo, the great Apache war chief, stopped here. *FYI:* Truth or Consequences Chamber of Commerce, 505-894-3536; or Geronimo's Spring, 505-894-6600.

2) Ojo Caliente: Named "Hot Spring," this area was colonized by Spaniards in the early eighteenth century, but it was already Ute and Comanche territory. Today, the recreational complex includes private and communal mineral baths, herbal wraps, massages, facials, a hotel-motel, a restaurant, and plenty of arsenic and lithium water to drink. (Some of Ojo is under reconstruction after a 1992 fire.) *FYI:* Hwy 285, north of Española; 505-583-2233.

3) Gila Hot Springs: There are camping and picnic facilities by the river's hot soaking pools. Gila Hot Springs Vacation Center offers guided hunting, fishing, and horseback trips. *FYI:* 4 miles below Gila Cliff Dwellings National Monument on Hwy 15; 505-536-9551.

4) Montezuma Hot Springs: These natural springs are located on private property a few miles northwest of Las Vegas near the site of the Montezuma Hotel. The hotel was built by the Atchison, Topeka, & Santa Fe Railroad to lure affluent tourists to the area. Its design is Queen Anne style, and it cost more than $200,000 to build in the 1880s. Although the hotel is now closed, the Armand Hammer World College of the American West opened on the property in 1982. Remember your manners: no nude bathing or beer cans, please. *FYI:* Armand Hammer World College, State Rd. 65; 505-454-4200. 🐾

Spirit Trivia

☞ **Truth or Consequences is the town of many names. It was declared the Province of San Felipe by Captain Francisco Sanchez Chamuscado in 1581. Hot Springs was the next moniker, bestowed in honor of nearby natural hot springs. Finally, in 1950, it became "T or C" in honor of the Ralph Edwards radio program. The show was so popular, it made the switch to television.**

The Santuario de Chimayo

Spirit Yourself Away

When you need to get away from it all, New Mexico has some great places where you can retreat from the world either alone or in a group of 2,500.

1) Monastery of Christ in the Desert: Benedictines specialize in making travelers feel welcome, and this settlement is no exception. Minute quarters are available at a nominal fee that includes meals. Guests are asked to contribute to their room and board by helping out with simple chores. The adobe, glass, stone, and wood chapel is of architectural note. The monastery is on the State Register of Cultural Properties. *FYI:* write Monastery of Christ in the Desert, Abiquiu, NM 87510.

2) Lama Foundation: Located near Taos, this 25-year-old foundation is the home of a year-round "intentional community," which means its members have come together with the intention of participating in community activities on a daily basis. During the summer months, Lama offers a series of ecumenical retreats and workshops that might include a permaculture design course, a vision quest, a meditation course, or Sufi dancing. The area is beautiful and inspiring. *FYI:* P.O. Box 240, San Cristobal, NM 87564; 505-586-1269.

3) Ghost Ranch Conference Center: This national study center of the Presbyterian church is situated on 21,000 scenic acres of a former dude ranch. Summer is the high season when workshops are offered on subjects ranging from theology to river rafting. The center is also an **Elderhostel** stop, and independent groups are welcome on a space available basis.

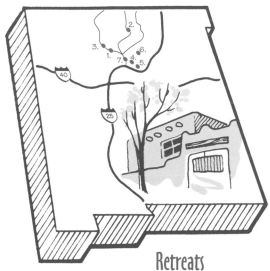

Retreats

Off-season is the best time to set up your own retreat; accommodations range from spartan casitas to simple hotellike rooms, and there is a dining hall. *FYI:* 65 miles north of Santa Fe on Hwy 84, mile marker 224; 505-685-4333 or 685-4334.

4) Glorieta Conference Center: What started forty years ago as a Baptist Assembly has grown into the largest conference center in the state, boasting a maximum capacity of 2,500. *FYI:* I-25 at Pecos exit; 505-757-6161.

5) Pecos River Ranch: This 2,000-acre business retreat along the Pecos River is part of entrepreneur Larry Wilson's vision. Although some of the program is geared to corporate use, schools, government organizations, and individuals take advantage of the facility and its empowerment and learning programs. The ranch retreat can handle up to 100 people and includes a gourmet restaurant, a swimming pool, tennis courts, and three outdoor jacuzzis with hillside views. *FYI:* about 35 miles east of Santa Fe; 505-989-9101.

6) Our Lady of Guadalupe Abbey: This is a coed monastery where monks, nuns, brothers, and committed laity live together year-round. In addition to guest rooms, a chapel, a meeting hall, and an office, the monastery also has its own publishing facility, Dove Publications. *FYI:* near Pecos; 505-757-6415.

7) Carmelite Monastery: This is a cloistered community where 11 nuns live in solitude. *FYI:* Santa Fe. 🔔

Tim Thompson

Healing Trivia

☞ The Santuario de Chimayó is famous for its 6-foot crucifix and the curative powers of Chimayó earth. Crutches, braces, locks of hair, and letters have been left by those who found strength and solace here. Before you visit, keep in mind that this is a place of worship, and tourist traffic can be intrusive.

☞ A famed shrine is located at the residence of the Rubio family in Lake Arthur because an image of Jesus Christ became visible to Mrs. Rubio on a flour tortilla on October 5, 1977.

☞ Sikhs of the East Indian religious tradition have their Western center just outside the city of Española.

"Chances that a resident of Santa Fe, New Mexico, is a 'healer' of some sort: 1 in 52." Harper's Index, 1987.

New Age Nouveau New Mexico

Tarot, numerology, intuitive consultations, astrology, and psychic surgery are all alternative ways to align your chakras, balance your aura, and heal the inner beast in New Mexico. Santa Fe is the state capital; it's also the nexus of the New Age. The city's Yellow Pages contain more than 35 listings under "Therapeutic Massage," at least 55 listings for "Acupuncturists" (including those who practice on horses, cats, and dogs), 15 entries under "Herbs," and 18 listings under "Holistic Practitioners."

What Credentials Tell You

In the area of mental health, New Mexico requires licenses for practicing psychiatrists, psychologists, and social workers only. A bill to license counselors is pending in Legislature. When you see advertisements for certified iridologists, kinesiologists, channelers, crystal healers, aroma therapists, reflexologists—etc.!—keep in mind that these particular certifications do not come from the state. On the one hand, certification may demonstrate hours of education and training. On the other hand, it might only mean that paper was sold for a fee. Before you place your well-being in the hands of a licensed or certified anything, ask questions! ❧

New Mexico's palm readers often hang a shingle to advertise their place of business. **Sister Rosa** has been interpreting palms in Santa Fe for at least a decade.

Tim Thompson

Sweat lodges made of juniper branches covered with skins or blankets and heated with hot rocks have been used in Native American ceremonies for centuries. Today, even New Mexico's state's penitentiary has a sweat lodge.

Old Age Healing

By the end of the nineteenth century, the dreaded White Plague, or tuberculosis, and its treatment dominated medicine in New Mexico. It brought hundreds of physicians to the state and influenced the development of area hospitals. In search of a cure, "Lungers" flocked to the arid climate, sunshine, and high elevations of "nature's sanatorium for consumptives."

Tubercular cures were varied and sometimes exotic. Besides taking rest and sunshine, victims were strapped into contraptions and then hung upside down, spun around, and jiggled here and there in extreme efforts to clear the lungs. But it wasn't until the advent of effective drug therapy in the 1940s and 1950s that the threat of consumption lessened.

The **Light Institute of Galisteo** was exposed to the world when Shirley MacLaine experienced some transformational spiritual healing here. Various facilitators will guide you through quadruple sessions to "clear imprints of multi-incarnation." If you don't know what this means, it may not be the therapy for you. *FYI:* HC-75, Box 50, Galisteo, NM 87540.

Certified Trivia

☛ **In 1992, more than 1,200 individuals qualified for state licensing as massage therapists. Requirements included 650 hours of schooling and passing state boards.**

☛ **In 1992, roughly 250 individuals were listed as state-licensed acupuncturists, which means they had at least 1,800 school hours and passed the state boards.**

Ghosties

New Mexico's ghosts are a mixed bunch. La Posada Hotel in Santa Fe may be haunted by an otherworldly interior decorator, the Plaza Hotel in Las Vegas appears to have multiple spirits wandering its halls, and La Llorona, the wailing woman (and the subject of numerous Mexican and southwestern Hispanic legends), is said to wander the desert moaning for the child she murdered. Although her cries are terrifying, the guilt-ridden and grief-stricken La Llorona isn't perceived as intending harm to the living. Instead, an encounter with the lady should be taken as a warning; it's time to reconsider your actions and reform your errant ways.

St. James Hotel, Cimarron

Mark Nohl, courtesy NM Magazine

Room 18 at the **St. James Hotel** in Cimarron is famous for its metaphysical occupant—the ghost of James Wright, a man who played one poker game too many. But additional ghosts may haunt the hotel, because gunman Clay Allison is thought to have killed more than 25 folks here. The St. James was restored in 1985 by Los Alamos scientist, Ed Sitzberger. The village of Cimarron (settled in 1844) was on the Mountain Branch of the Santa Fe Trail. Its present population is 888. *FYI:* Hwy 21 in Cimarron; 505-376-2664.

Lamy's **Legal Tender Restaurant** has two ghosts—a lady in white and a man in black. Should you spot either one when you visit, you are entitled to a complimentary beverage. Limit one ghost, one drink.

Tim Thompson

Legal Tender Restaurant and Saloon, Lamy

FYI: 20 miles south of Santa Fe on Hwy 285; 505-982-8425.

The ghost of early owner Byron T. Mills is said to rattle the floorboards of the **Plaza Hotel** in Las Vegas. This tall, odd-looking man ran the Plaza when it was a boardinghouse for Highlands University students. Apparently, he ran a strict house, knocking on doors, demanding quiet, and, sometimes, peeping over the transoms. Of late, Byron's spirit has been "felt" by staff members. (Since no portrait of Mills hangs in the hotel, it's difficult to know the ghost by sight.) A shadow may disappear into room 201, but when the night clerk unlocks the door, no one's there. By almost all versions, the Plaza ghost—male or female—is benevolent. One guest swore she was visited by a female spirit wearing peach blossom perfume. Another had a ghostly experience with chocolate. But usually, when guests mention the sound of knocking after dark, the management assumes it's old Byron, demanding quiet. *FYI:* on the Las Vegas Plaza; 505-425-3591.

On a walking **Ghost Tour** with Santa Fe's Southwest Adventure Tours, you'll learn about half a dozen of the capital city's legends and spirits. One of the more visible is the restless wife of a nineteeth-century German immigrant. Julie Schuster Staab wasn't too keen about relocating to a town of mud huts, so her husband built her a beautiful home Victorian-style. That home is now part of **La Posada de Santa Fe** hotel, and much of the historical interior has been left as is. Mrs. Staab died almost 100 years ago in what is now room 256, right above the bar. *FYI:* Santa Fe; 505-986-0000.

All Souls Day, November 2, has been celebrated in a variety of ways throughout the world. In Santa Fe, the **Dia de los Muertos** or Day of the Dead, is a time to commemorate ancestors and friends who have died. It's also a time to consider your feelings about The Great Unknown. *FYI:* Center for Contemporary Arts, 1050 Old Pecos Trail, Santa Fe; 505-982-1338.

Lost Treasure

Quivira was a city where the streets were paved with gold and people drank from golden goblets and bathed in golden tubs. At least, that's what ancient (and creaky) legends of the Southwest tell us. New Mexico has its share of newer legends, many of which deal with buried or hidden treasure.

The tale of the **Lost Padre Mine** often told in Las Cruces country concerns a fortune—millions in gold—hidden in the Organ Mountains about 200 years ago by a soldier who revealed his deathbed secret to a priest. Years later, the priest, known as Father LaRue, led his village in search of the treasure because a drought had ruined their crops. After LaRue and his followers discovered gold, they mined and stored great quantities for years. When officials of the church realized they had lost contact with Father LaRue, they sent an emissary, Maximo Milliano, from Mexico. Milliano managed to find the villagers and their priest after a year of trekking around the country-side. When LaRue and friends refused to hand over the treasure, they were (a) tortured and/or (b) killed, and the secret was never revealed. According to some versions of the story, the gold was roughly two days' journey from the Paso del Norte and hidden near San Agustín Pass, where a spring flowed by a very high cliff.

Out of this World

Nineteen-hundred-forty-seven was a big year for **UFOs** in New Mexico. Newspapers from the time are filled with stories of saucer sightings in Albuquerque, Socorro, Pope, and Silver City. Some folks believe a spacecraft maneuvered by aliens left debris  on a farm outside Roswell and crash-landed on the St. Augustín Plains that same year. The possibility of a government cover-up, top-secret research, and alien bodies in storage have been explored in numerous books, articles, and television shows. After all, it was a dark and stormy night. *FYI:* UFO Museum; 505-625-9495.

The town of Roswell had its beginnings in the late 1800s as a watering hole for the Pecos Valley stock drives. In the 1930s, liquid fuel rocket flights were conducted here by Robert Goddard. Roswell Museum and Art Center features a re-creation of Goddard's rocket testing workshop. *FYI:* Roswell visitors' information; 505-623-5695.

Unsolved Mysteries

Coller Collection. #C2320 NM Records Center & Archives

Pancho Villa

☞ Could Mexican revolutionary Pancho Villa have stashed a stockpile of weapons and supplies near the summit of Providence Cone to the west of Las Cruces? That's the story according to some treasure hounds; Villa thought he would need supplies after his raid on Columbus, New Mexico, on March 9, 1916. Because Pancho Villa was pursued into Mexico by Gen. John J. "Black Jack" Pershing, he never made it as far as his stash, and presumably, it's still there. If you believe that, you're a treasure hunter at heart.

☞ Treasure discovered by Milton C. Noss in 1937 has made the pages of *Time* and *Newsweek*. The booty, said to be worth billions, was rehidden by Noss at Victorio Peak.

☞ During the 1970s, the mutilated bodies of cattle began showing up on remote New Mexico ranchlands. Often, the sexual organs, lips, tongue, and eyes had been cut out and the carcass was drained of blood. Was it the work of extraterrestrials? Thousands of dollars and an organized investigation didn't prove yea or nay. There are those who still believe that visitors from space did the surgery; others credit natural predators.

KIDS' ADVENTURES

Old Coal Mine Museum: You can explore three browsable acres crammed with rusty reminders of the good old days (even if you don't remember them). Museum highlights include a 1919 Model T pickup truck, a 1929 International dump truck, and an actual coal seam in the mine shaft itself. *FYI:* Main St., Madrid, NM 87010; 505-473-0743.

Turquoise Trail Theater Company: Melodramas are a specialty on weekends in the summer season. You're free to boo and hiss to your heart's content. *FYI:* Main St., Madrid; 505-984-6760.

El Rancho de las Golondrinas: The Ranch of the Swallows is the perfect place to spread out, have fun, and learn at the same time. Listen to music, stroll the countryside, and sample brown bread pulled hot from traditional hornos (outdoor ovens). *FYI:* 15 miles south of Santa Fe, exit 271 from I-25; 505-471-2261.

Fish Hatcheries: Dexter National Fish Hatchery (located along Pecos River east of Dexter) is a center for research and rearing of endemic endangered fish species. Visitors are invited to tour the facility. FYI: P.O. Box 219, Dexter, NM 88230; 505-734-5910. The **Mescalero Fish Hatchery** is situated in the high country of the Mescalero Apache Reservation. Visitors are welcome to view the trout tanks. Lunkers have their very own raceways. *FYI:* P.O. Box 247, Mescalero, NM 88340; 505-671-4401.

Ghost Ranch Living Museum: The Southwest's native flora and fauna are on view in outdoor exhibits. Self-guided and guided tours, lectures, and films are all part of the show. *FYI:* north of Abiquiu on US84; 505-685-4312.

Shiprock: This is a sight sure to fill you with awe no matter your age. In the Navajo language, Shiprock, or "Tse Bida Hi," means "rock with wings." Rising 1,700 feet above the plains, this massive volcanic rock figures in Navajo mythology as the great bird that carried the ancients from the north. Tread softly here; Shiprock is sacred to many. *FYI:* 37 miles west of Farmington near the Arizona/New Mexico border.

Playing with magnets at the Santa Fe Children's Museum

Santa Fe Children's Museum: The exhibits are hands-on, exciting, and challenging. Subjects covered include sciences and humanities. *FYI:* 1050 Old Pecos Trail, Santa Fe; 505-989-8359.

Bandelier National Monument: Kid-sized cliff dwellings make this a great place for smaller people to burn off steam. Ladders and tight squeezes abound. Visitors center and facilities. *FYI:* near Los Alamos, off NM4; 505-672-3861.

Museum of International Folk Art: This museum houses the world's largest collection of international folk art. The Hispanic Heritage Wing makes this the nation's most important museum of Hispanic folk art. *FYI:* 706 Camino Lejo, Santa Fe; 505-827-6350.

Museum of Indian Arts and Culture: The exhibits focus on Pueblo, Navajo, and Apache Native Americans. A Living Traditions program features Indian artisans at work—basketry, pottery, weaving, bead-work, and jewelry. *FYI:* 710 Camino Lejo, Santa Fe; 505-827-6344.

Shakespeare in the Park: Free productions are a family affair. They run throughout August and September, outdoors, in Santa Fe. *FYI:* P.O. Box 2188, Santa Fe, NM 87504; Santa Fe visitors information, 505-984-6760 or 800-777-CITY.

Rio Grande Zoological Park: 1,200 animals from around the world fill these acres. Favorites include a children's zoo and special reptile and amphibian exhibits as well as a prairie dog park. Zoo personnel are kind, concerned, and informed. *FYI:* 903 Tenth St. SW, Albuquerque; 505-843-7413.

Santa Fe Ski Area Little Chipmunk Corner: This newish children's complex has its own lunchroom and rest room facilities. The staff can handle infants 2 months and older if arrangements are made in advance. *FYI:* Ski Basin Rd., Santa Fe; 505-988-9636.

New Mexico State Fair: This is the eighth largest in the nation. There's the midway, Indian and Spanish villages, recording stars, pigs, cows, horses, quarter horse racing, PRCA rodeo, arts and crafts, baked goods— you name it! Begins the Friday after Labor Day for 17 days. *FYI:* State Fairgrounds, P.O. Box 8546, Albuquerque, NM 87198; 505-265-1791.

Living Desert State Park: You can see birds, mountain lions, deer, snakes, and javelina—all in their natural habitat. The park is situated in the Ocotillo Hills above Carlsbad. Persons 6 years and under are admitted free. *FYI:* south of Carlsbad off US62/180; 505-887-5516.

Alamogordo Space Center/International Space Hall of Fame will make you think of moonscapes and extraterrestrials. *FYI:* Alamogordo; 505-437-2840 or 800-545-4021.

Las Cruces Farmers and Crafts Market: Check out the fresh veggies, listen to music, watch the toy demonstrations, or throw a major munch. This market has been in business for more than two decades, and it's now a permanent part of the Las Cruces Downtown Mall on Wednesdays and Saturdays. *FYI:* Las Cruces visitors information; 505-524-8521 or 800-FIESTAS.

All Species Day is a celebration of all the world's living creatures. It happens almost every May in Santa Fe. Parades, costumes, dancing, food, and information booths are all part of the fun. *FYI:* Santa Fe visitors information; 505-984-6760 or 800-777-CITY.

The **Corrales Harvest Festival** has music, food, and fun as well as a juried arts and crafts fair. This annual October event attracts thousands of folks from Albuquerque and surrounding areas. *FYI:* Albuquerque visitors information, 505-243-3696 or 800-284-2282. ❧

INDEX

Other Books from John Muir Publications

Adventure Vacations: From Trekking in New Guinea to Swimming in Siberia, Bangs 256 pp. $17.95

Asia Through the Back Door, 3rd ed., Steves and Gottberg 326 pp. $15.95

Belize: A Natural Destination, Mahler, Wotkyns, Schafer 304 pp. $16.95

Bus Touring: Charter Vacations, U.S.A., Warren with Bloch 168 pp. $9.95

California Public Gardens: A Visitor's Guide, Sigg 304 pp. $16.95

Costa Rica: A Natural Destination, 2nd ed., Sheck 288 pp. $16.95

Elderhostels: The Students' Choice, 2nd ed., Hyman 312 pp. $15.95

Environmental Vacations: Volunteer Projects to Save the Planet, 2nd ed., Ocko 248 pp. $16.95

Europe 101: History & Art for the Traveler, 4th ed., Steves and Openshaw 372 pp. $15.95

Europe Through the Back Door, 11th ed., Steves 448 pp. $17.95

Europe Through the Back Door Phrase Book: French, Steves 112 pp. $4.95

Europe Through the Back Door Phrase Book: German, Steves 112 pp. $4.95

Europe Through the Back Door Phrase Book: Italian, Steves 112 pp. $4.95

Floating Vacations: River, Lake, and Ocean Adventures, White 256 pp. $17.95

A Foreign Visitor's Survival Guide to America, Baldwin and Levine 224 pp. $12.95

Great Cities of Eastern Europe, Rapoport 256 pp. $16.95

Guatemala: A Natural Destination, Mahler 288 pp. $16.95

Gypsying After 40: A Guide to Adventure and Self-Discovery, Harris 264 pp. $14.95

The Heart of Jerusalem, Nellhaus 336 pp. $12.95

Indian America: A Traveler's Companion, 2nd ed., Eagle/Walking Turtle 448 pp. $17.95

Interior Furnishings Southwest: The Sourcebook of the Best Production Craftspeople, Deats and Villani 256 pp. $19.95

Mona Winks: Self-Guided Tours of Europe's Top Museums, 2nd ed., Steves and Openshaw 456 pp. $16.95

Opera! The Guide to Western Europe's Great Houses, Zietz 296 pp. $18.95

Paintbrushes and Pistols: How the Taos Artists Sold the West, Taggett and Schwarz 280 pp. $17.95

The People's Guide to Mexico, 9th ed., Franz 608 pp. $18.95

The People's Guide to RV Camping in Mexico, Franz with Rogers 320 pp. $13.95

Ranch Vacations: The Complete Guide to Guest and Resort, Fly-Fishing, and Cross-Country Skiing Ranches, 2nd ed., Kilgore 396 pp. $18.95

The Shopper's Guide to Art and Crafts in the Hawaiian Islands, Schuchter 272 pp. $13.95

The Shopper's Guide to Mexico, Rogers and Rosa 224 pp. $9.95

Ski Tech's Guide to Equipment, Skiwear, and Accessories, ed. Tanler 144 pp. $11.95

Ski Tech's Guide to Maintenance and Repair, ed. Tanler 160 pp. $11.95

A Traveler's Guide to Asian Culture, Chambers 224 pp. $13.95

Traveler's Guide to Healing Centers and Retreats in North America, Rudee and Blease 240 pp. $11.95

Understanding Europeans, Miller 272 pp. $14.95

Undiscovered Islands of the Caribbean, 3nd ed., Willes 264 pp. $14.95

Undiscovered Islands of the Mediterranean, 2nd ed., Moyer and Willes 256 pp. $13.95

Undiscovered Islands of the U.S. and Canadian West Coast, Moyer and Willes 208 pp. $12.95

A Viewer's Guide to Art: A Glossary of Gods, People, and Creatures, Shaw and Warren 144 pp. $10.95

The Visitor's Guide to the Birds of the Eastern National Parks: United States and Canada, Wauer 400 pp. $15.95

2 to 22 Days Series
Each title offers 22 flexible daily itineraries that can be used to get the most out of vacations of any length. Included are not only "must see" attractions but also little-known villages and hidden "jewels" as well as valuable general information.

22 Days Around the World, 1993 ed., Rapoport and Willes 264 pp. $13.95

2 to 22 Days Around the Great Lakes, 1993 ed., Schuchter 192 pp. $10.95

22 Days in Alaska, Lanier 128 pp. $7.95

2 to 22 Days in the American Southwest, 1993 ed., Harris 176 pp. $10.95

2 to 22 Days in Asia, 1993 ed., Rapoport and Willes 176 pp. $10.95

2 to 22 Days in Australia, 1993 ed., Gottberg 192 pp. $10.95

2 to 22 Days in California, 1993 ed., Rapoport 192 pp. $10.95

22 Days in China, Duke and Victor 144 pp. $7.95

2 to 22 Days in Europe, 1993 ed., Steves 288 pp. $13.95

2 to 22 Days in Florida, 1993 ed., Harris 192 pp. $10.95

2 to 22 Days in France, 1993 ed., Steves 192 pp. $10.95

2 to 22 Days in Germany, Austria, & Switzerland, 1993 ed., Steves 224 pp. $10.95

2 to 22 Days in Great Britain, 1993 ed., Steves 192 pp. $10.95

2 to 22 Days in Hawaii, 1993 ed., Schuchter 176 pp. $10.95

22 Days in India, Mathur 136 pp. $7.95

22 Days in Japan, Old 136 pp. $7.95

22 Days in Mexico, 2nd ed., Rogers and Rosa 128 pp. $7.95

2 to 22 Days in New England, 1993 ed., Wright 192 pp. $10.95

2 to 22 Days in New Zealand, 1993 ed., Schuchter 192 pp. $10.95

2 to 22 Days in Norway, Sweden, & Denmark, 1993 ed., Steves 192 pp. $10.95

2 to 22 Days in the Pacific Northwest, 1993 ed., Harris 192 pp. $10.95

2 to 22 Days in the Rockies, 1993 ed., Rapoport 192 pp. $10.95

2 to 22 Days in Spain & Portugal, 1992 ed., Steves 192 pp. $9.95

2 to 22 Days in Texas, 1993 ed., Harris 192 pp. $10.95

2 to 22 Days in Thailand, 1993 ed., Richardson 180 pp. $10.95

22 Days in the West Indies, Morreale and Morreale 136 pp. $7.95

Parenting Series

Being a Father: Family, Work, and Self, *Mothering* Magazine 176 pp. $12.95
Preconception: A Woman's Guide to Preparing for Pregnancy and Parenthood, Aikey-Keller 232 pp. $14.95
Schooling at Home: Parents, Kids, and Learning, *Mothering* Magazine 264 pp. $14.95
Teens: A Fresh Look, *Mothering* Magazine 240 pp. $14.95

"Kidding Around" Travel Guides for Young Readers

Written for kids eight years of age and older.
Kidding Around Atlanta, Pedersen 64 pp. $9.95
Kidding Around Boston, 2nd ed., Byers 64 pp. $9.95
Kidding Around Chicago, 2nd ed., Davis 64 pp. $9.95
Kidding Around the Hawaiian Islands, Lovett 64 pp. $9.95
Kidding Around London, Lovett 64 pp. $9.95
Kidding Around Los Angeles, Cash 64 pp. $9.95
Kidding Around the National Parks of the Southwest, Lovett 108 pp. $12.95
Kidding Around New York City, 2nd ed., Lovett 64 pp. $9.95
Kidding Around Paris, Clay 64 pp. $9.95
Kidding Around Philadelphia, Clay 64 pp. $9.95
Kidding Around San Diego, Luhrs 64 pp. $9.95
Kidding Around San Francisco, Zibart 64 pp. $9.95
Kidding Around Santa Fe, York 64 pp. $9.95
Kidding Around Seattle, Steves 64 pp. $9.95
Kidding Around Spain, Biggs 108 pp. $12.95
Kidding Around Washington, D.C., 2nd ed., Pedersen 64 pp. $9.95

"Extremely Weird" Series for Young Readers

Written for kids eight years of age and older.
Extremely Weird Bats, Lovett 48 pp. $9.95
Extremely Weird Birds, Lovett 48 pp. $9.95
Extremely Weird Endangered Species, Lovett 48 pp. $9.95
Extremely Weird Fishes, Lovett 48 pp. $9.95
Extremely Weird Frogs, Lovett 48 pp. $9.95
Extremely Weird Insects, Lovett 48 pp. $9.95
Extremely Weird Primates, Lovett 48 pp. $9.95
Extremely Weird Reptiles, Lovett 48 pp. $9.95
Extremely Weird Sea Creatures, Lovett 48 pp. $9.95
Extremely Weird Spiders, Lovett 48 pp. $9.95

Masters of Motion Series

For kids eight years and older.
How to Drive an Indy Race Car, Rubel 48 pages $9.95
How to Fly a 747, Paulson 48 pages $9.95
How to Fly the Space Shuttle, Shorto 48 pages $9.95

Quill Hedgehog Adventures Series

Green fiction for kids. Written for kids eight years of age and older.
Quill's Adventures in the Great Beyond. Waddington-Feather 96 pp. $5.95
Quill's Adventures in Wasteland, Waddington-Feather 132 pp. $5.95
Quill's Adventures in Grozzieland, Waddington-Feather 132 pp. $5.95

X-ray Vision Series

For kids eight years and older.
Looking Inside Cartoon Animation, Schultz 48 pages $9.95
Looking Inside Sports Aerodynamics, Schultz 48 pages $9.95
Looking Inside Sunken Treasure, Schultz 48 pp. $9.95
Looking Inside Telescopes and the Night Sky, Schultz 48 pp. $9.95
Looking Inside the Brain, Schultz 48 pages $9.95

Other Young Readers Titles

Habitats: Where the Wild Things Live, Hacker & Kaufman 48 pp. $9.95
The Indian Way: Learning to Communicate with Mother Earth, McLain 114 pp. $9.95
The Kids' Environment Book: What's Awry and Why, Pedersen 192 pp. $13.95
Kids Explore America's African-American Heritage, Westridge Young Writers Workshop 112 pp. $8.95
Kids Explore America's Hispanic Heritage, Westridge Young Writers Workshop 112 pp. $7.95
Rads, Ergs, and Cheeseburgers: The Kids' Guide to Energy and the Environment, Yanda 108 pp. $12.95

Automotive Titles

How to Keep Your VW Alive, 15th ed., 464 pp. $21.95
How to Keep Your Subaru Alive 480 pp. $21.95
How to Keep Your Toyota Pickup Alive 392 pp. $21.95
How to Keep Your Datsun/Nissan Alive 544 pp. $21.95
The Greaseless Guide to Car Care Confidence: Take the Terror Out of Talking to Your Mechanic, Jackson 224 pp. $14.95
Off-Road Emergency Repair & Survival, Ristow 160 pp. $9.95

Ordering Information

If you cannot find our books in your local bookstore, you can order directly from us. If you send us money for a book not yet available, we will hold your money until we can ship you the book. Your books will be sent to you via UPS (for U.S. destinations). UPS will not deliver to a P.O. Box; please give us a street address. Include $3.75 for the first item ordered and $.50 for each additional item to cover shipping and handling costs. For airmail within the U.S., enclose $4.00. All foreign orders will be shipped surface rate; please enclose $3.00 for the first item and $1.00 for each additional item. Please inquire about foreign airmail rates.

Method of Payment

Your order may be paid by check, money order, or credit card. We cannot be responsible for cash sent through the mail. All payments must be made in U.S. dollars drawn on a U.S. bank. Canadian postal money orders in U.S. dollars are acceptable. For VISA, MasterCard, or American Express orders, include your card number, expiration date, and your signature, or call (800) 888-7504. Books ordered on American Express cards can be shipped only to the billing address of the cardholder. Sorry, no C.O.D.'s. Residents of sunny New Mexico, add 5.875% tax to the total.

Address all orders and inquiries to:
John Muir Publications
P.O. Box 613
Santa Fe, NM 87504
(505) 982-4078
(800) 888-7504